HOPE *of the* NATION

This lovely volume has been made available by generous citizens concerned with upholding Judeo-Christian values. In appreciating these values and in respecting the generosity of these local citizens, **PLEASE DO NOT REMOVE THIS VOLUME FROM THIS ROOM**.

Hope of the Nation has been placed here so that patients can enjoy its beauty and inspiration. Please honor the book's content and purpose by not removing it from this room.

Should you wish to order a personal copy, you may call (800) 275-6008. Thank you for your cooperation.

Sincerely,
The Publishers

**PLEASE DO NOT REMOVE THIS
VOLUME FROM THE AREA.
THANK YOU!**

HOPE *of the* NATION

is provided for your reading pleasure
by the concerned community leaders listed below.

HOPE *of the* NATION

Good Will Publishers, Inc. Copyright © 1993

ACKNOWLEDGMENTS

ORIGINAL ART

George Malick is recognized as one of the finest artists in the American tradition. Commissioned by the Rockwell Museum to paint Norman Rockwell's portrait following the popular artist's death, he was also commissioned to reproduce in oils several Rockwell charcoals. Many of the Rockwell collection plates were actually painted by Mr. Malick. Particularly admired of Mr. Malick's work are the outstanding oil paintings of scenes and characters of the Old and New Testaments as portrayed in this volume. The editor wishes to express his sincere gratitude for Mr. Malick's continued relationship with Good Will Publishers, Inc.

PHOTOGRAPHIC

The editor also wishes to express many thanks to the following for their contributions to the photographic section of this volume: Dorothy Holland, Emily and Allison Smith, Haskel Currence, Kimberly, Stephanie and David Ramsey, Diane Hoefling, J. C. Carothers, William Craig, Louise Hair, Charlotte Mahannah, Fred Haithcox, Harold Guffey, Matthew Courtney, Yonette Ninneman, Lakitia Hulon, Cindy Elmore, Raymond Butler, Sandra McDougal, Patricia Clinton, Eppert Lowery, Michelle Kent, Rabbi Leah Benamy, Fern Beigh, Catherine Gardner, Steve Romito, Jeffrey Dawkins, Betty Fairfax, Binh and Lisa Dang, Anh Nguyen, Lam, Khanh, Tuan and Hoang Tran, Reverend Francis O'Rourke, Gloria Butler, Warren Clark, the Library of Congress, NASA Jet Propulsion Labs, Office to the Assistant Secretary of Defense. A very special thanks to the Gallagher family, the Brunnemer family, Jon Silla and Richard Haithcox.

PRODUCTION

Many thanks to Lewis Holland for his knowledge, experience and support which stand behind the creation of this work.

TYPESET, LAYOUT AND DESIGN

This volume would never have been possible without the dedicated work of Ron Mahannah, whose commitment to excellence is evident throughout.

EDITORIAL

The editor, Fred G. Gallagher, wishes to express his sincerest gratitude to R. M. Gallagher and J. P. Bradley for close attention to the principles embraced by this book.

HOPE *of the* NATION

OUR AMERICAN HERITAGE

INTRODUCTION

If the history of the United States is anything, it is a record of human response; of human beings impassioned by the pursuit of truth, liberty and individual destiny; of human beings seeking expression of their innermost yearnings; yearnings to do good and avoid evil, to create families, communities and a nation free of oppression. The history of the United States is a record of that effort, which is an effort to reach beyond the limitations of human weakness and to follow and apply within the realm of family and society, the will of God.

And thus the laws of states and the nation came into being as collective notions of right and wrong behavior. These notions were based upon objective standards of conduct passed down through the centuries. But how did these standards arrive in our New World consciousness? In point of fact, they were the standards that veered the course of western civilization from pagan domination and its attendant debasement of human life toward a new vision of a humankind capable of elevated moral action, great faith and commitment to justice and mercy–the standards brought forth by the Judeo-Christian Tradition.

Judeo-Christian standards are objective. That is to say, we do not decide what they are. God, our Creator, who made us and gave us our life, decides what they are and subsequently how we should conduct our lives. The core of the Judeo-Christian standards is the Ten Commandments. They were given to us by God in the Old Testament, lived out in human response by the heroes and heroines therein, endorsed by New Testament characters who struggled to know and obey the Son of God, and brought to fruition by Jesus Christ Himself who said, ''I have come, not to destroy the law, but to perfect it.'' Churches and synagogues throughout the centuries have constantly taught these core standards, and have also taught rules of human conduct that are necessary to protect them.

It is with this appreciation of how Judeo-Christian standards unfolded in the lives of the people of scripture and in the life of Christ, who is the perfection of those standards that we present this volume. Its title, *Hope of the Nation*, is meant to put forth the proposition that only a return to these objective standards of conduct will return our nation to greatness. When standards become subjective, we lose a common code of behavior, a touchstone of moral action. And with the disintegration of moral codes comes the inevitable devaluation of human life and the subsequent debasement and destruction of our American way of life. This process has already begun. Every day, felons are released early from prisons as there is no room to keep them. This is due to the enormous increase in murder, rape and other forms of violence. Corruption in business and government threatens to destroy our economy. Since 1963, 10 to 14-year-old girls' pregnancies rose 533 percent, and the institution of marriage and family are being attacked from all sides. The moral fabric of our nation is unraveling.

But for most of its history, the United States

sought to conduct its affairs in accordance with the Judeo-Christian standards so clearly endorsed by its founders. At times it strayed from these standards, but the standards were there and acknowledged, allowing us to correct our failures. The fundamental standard, or value, and the essential source of all the other standards, was the recognition of God, our Creator. As Thomas Jefferson said, ''God who gave us life gave us liberty. Can the liberties of a nation be secure when we have removed a conviction that these liberties are the gift of God?'' There is an abundance of evidence that the United States was founded on objective Judeo-Christian standards. Let's look first of all at the Declaration of Independence, often said to be the most important of all American historical documents. ''We hold these truths to be self-evident that all men are created equal and are endowed by *their Creator* with certain inalienable rights.'' The rights the document is referring to are, of course, the right to life, liberty and the pursuit of happiness. This fundamentally important document leaves us in no doubt that God the Creator, God the Supreme Legislator of the moral law, is central in the thinking of the founders of this nation. The document goes on to state: ''we, therefore, appealing to the Supreme Judge of the world for the rectitude of our intentions...'' The founders here ask God, the Supreme Judge of the world, the judge of what is right and what is wrong, to guide them so that they will do what is right in

establishing this new nation.

A ten-year study of the Political Science Department of the University of Houston collected 15,000 pieces of writings of the founders to discover where they got their ideas. Of these, the researchers selected 3,152 pieces that they believed had the greatest impact on America's foundation. They discovered that the three men most quoted were Sir William Blackstone, an English jurist, Baron Montesquieu, a French political thinker, and John Locke, an English political thinker. These three had valuable political insights to offer. But the researchers were surprised to find that the Bible was quoted 16 times more often than these three men. In total, they found that 94 percent of the founders' quotes came directly or indirectly from the Bible!

In *Hope of the Nation*, we celebrate the Judeo-Christian Tradition through striking portraits of outstanding men, women and children of the Old Testament, through those in the New Testament who encountered the Son of God, our Lord Jesus Christ on earth, and through a pictorial exploration of the American way of life as it reflects the core standards of this Tradition. We are at a turning point in history, in the record of human response to the God of our forefathers. A response which reflects the objective, moral standards flowing forth from the Judeo-Christian Tradition is our only hope. To return to these standards is truly the hope of the nation.

OUR JUDEO-CHRISTIAN HERITAGE

BELIEVING IN GOD: THE STORY OF THE CHOSEN PEOPLE

Throughout the long history of humanity, there have been individuals who rose up to lead us to a better and righteous life. They were called rebels, for they rebelled against the worship of false gods and the resulting horror of injustice, hate, corruption and war. For their beliefs, they often experienced great suffering and sorrow; but, like the ensuing examples from the Old Testament of men and women who faced and overcame their trials, they felt they were chosen by God to labor for justice, brotherhood and a way of life which would reflect their commitment to moral standards.

If we are to cultivate the principles upon which our nation was founded and fulfill the destiny God wills for us, it behooves us to study the lives of others whose commitment to those principles have made their names immortal. And by examining our own lives and searching our own hearts in light of theirs, we may be able to determine how we can best serve God and our fellow human beings. God does not force us to serve Him; but, as Americans, He has given us, through a democratic system founded upon Judeo-Christian standards, a great opportunity to positively influence all of humanity.

THE PIONEER FATHER

Abraham

Abraham is the father of the Hebrew people. He is the first person in Scripture to break away from paganism and formulate the belief in One God. His greatness rests on the belief that a Supreme Being created the Universe and that this belief can elevate men's actions.

Abraham trusted in God; he had faith that God would help him when his own limited ability and understanding were not sufficient. And when he was put to the great test, to sacrifice his beloved son, Isaac, Abraham was prepared to obey because he had faith. And thereby was Isaac saved by the Lord.

As Abraham's belief in One God made him a pioneer, it also gave him values to live by. He felt that faith in God must be expressed in action. For this reason, it is said, Abraham pitched his tent at the crossroads with an entrance at each side. Whenever a wayfarer approached, it was to the front of the tent and he was invited to partake of the hospitality of Abraham's household.

An inner confidence helped Abraham break with the past and challenge the unknown, just as the early pioneers of America did. Those who built our great nation went forth like Abraham with the notion of establishing something better for their descendants. The America whose shores represent freedom to so many from distant lands recalls the great hospitality of our pioneer father, Abraham.

A WOMAN'S FAITH AND TRUST

Abraham was very old. He was worried about his son Isaac, now grown to manhood and still unmarried. He must find for Isaac a suitable wife from among their own people. Abraham, therefore, summoned a trusted servant and instructed him to seek a wife for Isaac.

Abraham's servant rested by the well in the village of Nahor in Mesopotamia. He prayed to God for help in his mission. "Give me a sign revealing Your will, O Lord. I will ask a damsel for a drink. If she does so, and also offers to water my camels, I will regard her as Your choice as Isaac's wife." Scarcely had he finished his prayer when Rebekah, "very fair to look upon, a virgin," came to the well. He asked her for a drink, and she immediately poured some water from her pitcher and gave it to him. Before he had time to thank her, she suggested that she draw

Isaac and Rebekah

water for his camels.

In Rebekah's home Abraham's servant explained his mission to her family, and related how God had answered his prayer for a sign. The family asked Rebekah if she would consent to marry Isaac. Convinced that God has revealed His will in answering the servant's prayer, Rebekah replied firmly, "I will go."

Rebekah's life-long dedication to the will of God shows her to be a woman of remarkable faith and trust. In today's world, where the American woman's role in society is undergoing great changes, it is difficult for many women to make decisions about their path in life. Faith and trust in God, our source of divine guidance, can be their greatest help in making these decisions.

UNITY AND SERVICE

As Rebekah rested in her tent, She thought, ''How different my twin sons are! Esau, like his father, is independent and full of daring. Jacob, like me, is affectionate and interested in others.'' She knew that Jacob would make a better leader for their tribe than his older brother.

The next day, Rebekah said to Jacob, ''Your father has sent Esau hunting. When Esau returns, he is going to make him the next leader of our tribe.'' Rebekah, taking advantage of Isaac's blindness dressed Jacob in Esau's clothes. Esau's skin was hairy, and Jacob's smooth, so Rebekah put goatskins on Jacob's hands and neck. Then she cooked a meal which Jacob brought to his father. Isaac noted that Jacob did not sound like Esau; but upon touching the hair on Jacob's hands, his doubts disappeared. And so, Isaac blessed Jacob and made him the next leader of the tribe.

When Esau found out what happened, he wanted to kill Jacob. So Rebekah sent Jacob to Haran to live with his uncle Laban. One night during the journey, Jacob dreamt of a great ladder reaching up to the heavens with angels going up and down on it. In the dream God promised Jacob and his descendants the land upon which he lay.

In Haran, Jacob worked for Laban whose daughter, Rachel,

Jacob and Esau

he married. He became rich and had twelve sons.

Years later, upon returning home to Canaan, Jacob met his brother Esau. To his great joy he found that Esau no longer hated him, and the two brothers embraced and wept for joy at seeing each other again.

Jacob became head of his tribe after the death of his father Isaac and went on to become the leader of a great nation.

Even after deception and trickery in the family, Jacob was willing to follow the will of God and Esau was willing to forgive. As the American family suffers the trials of modern culture, we would do well to look to Jacob and Esau as models of unity and service to God.

GENEROUS BROTHER, LOYAL SON

Jacob had twelve sons, but young Joseph was his favorite. The more Jacob showed his love for Joseph, as when he gave him the coat of many colors, the more jealous Jacob's other sons became. This, along with Joseph's dream that he would some day be their ruler, served to heap more hot coals upon the evil designs of his already vindictively jealous brothers.

One day, some traders came by, and Joseph's brothers seized the opportunity for vengeance by selling Joseph into slavery for twenty pieces of silver. When they returned home, they told Jacob that Joseph had been killed by wild beasts.

The traders took Joseph to Egypt where eventually he was imprisoned. While in prison, Joseph became known as an interpreter of dreams, and when the Pharaoh was greatly troubled by his dreams, it was suggested that he consult with Joseph.

Delighted with Joseph's explanation, the Pharaoh made him governor of all Egypt. And because Joseph administered wisely, Egypt came to have a great supply of grain, while surrounding countries were suffering famine. When Joseph's brothers came looking for food, Joseph showed them no bitterness. Instead he instructed them to bring Jacob to Egypt and settle under his kindly protection. Joseph is remembered as a wise, kind and forgiving man.

Joseph reunited with Jacob

Kindness and generosity have long been ideals cherished by Americans. Joseph's example is played out again and again in American history, but a great instance on a national scale would be the European Recovery Program, commonly referred to as the Marshall Plan. In April 1948 President Truman signed an act to administer the program which was to eventually disperse over $12 billion in aid to a war-wracked Europe. With the Soviet Union and others strongly opposing the plan, the United States stood like Joseph, kind, responsible and generous.

THE MODEL OF LEADERSHIP

Born in Egypt of Jewish parents, Moses grew to adulthood in the palace of the Pharaoh. The incident that saved his life, when the Pharaoh's daughter plucked him from the reeds where his mother had hidden him, also saved the Jewish people from extinction. His royal upbringing gave Moses the bearing and training for leadership. This, combined with his gentle nature, his great ability, and his identification with his people, enabled him to mold abject slaves into a disciplined and cohesive group that has survived for approximately four thousand years and has made boundless contributions to civilization.

When the Almighty summoned Moses to labor on behalf of His enslaved people, he felt he must respond affirmatively, even though it would mean separation from his wife and two sons.

At first, Moses was reluctant to accept his task. He felt inadequate. He stuttered and feared the people would not accept his authority.

Many times Moses despaired that his mission could not succeed. Often treated shabbily by the people, he prayed to God to relieve him of responsibility for them. But no matter how they fell short of his hopes for them, Moses never deserted his people.

As soon as Moses freed the Jews from Egyptian bondage, he bound them to the rule of law at Mount Sinai. Then he supervised them in the construction of their first House of God, for without awe for the Creator of the Universe there could be no reverence for life and no just society.

The combination of religion and law was Moses' monumental contribution to mankind. By weaving these two civilizing influences together—law for safety and stability; religion for inspiration and change—Moses prepared the former slaves to forge themselves into a well-knit, dynamic group with unlimited ability to adapt to the uncharted future.

Our founding fathers surely knew the contribution of Moses as they emulated him in their insistence upon the freedom to express their religious beliefs. Moses knew that the law was empty without moral substance. Indeed, the Ten Commandments have provided countless societies throughout history with the foundation of responsible government.

Moses with the tablets

WHITHER THOU GOEST...

All that is meant by love and faithfulness is personified in the character of Ruth. She had married a young Jew who came to Moab with his family when famine struck in Judah. Ten years had passed and Ruth had no children. Now, suddenly, Ruth's husband was dead, and she was left with his grief-stricken widowed mother, Naomi, who had lost another son in Moab. Naomi now wished only to return to Judah to live out her days.

Although Naomi counseled her to remain in Moab with her own people, Ruth insisted: "Entreat me not to leave thee, and to turn from following after thee; for whither thou goest, I will go." Ruth now renewed her vow, "Thy people shall be my people, and thy God, my God."

The decision to remain with Naomi and to cast her lot with the Jewish people gave Ruth immortal honor. For when the time of mourning was over and spring harvest came again, Ruth said to Naomi, "Let me now go to the field and glean among the ears of corn after him in whose sight I shall find favor." There she met Boaz and, with Naomi's blessing, Ruth became his wife, and a mother in Israel—ultimately the great-grandmother of King David.

Ruth knew the value and importance of family, and she remained loyal not only to her adopted religion, but also to her grieving mother-in-law. As we begin to see the disintegration of the American family, it would be wise to look to Ruth and honor the memory of her great virtue. Her loyalty led ultimately to a fruitful new life and a permanent place of honor in Jewish history. Great rewards also wait for those who remain loyal to the Judeo-Christian standards that are our heritage.

Ruth and Boaz

MOTHER OF ISRAEL

A woman of keen mind, great courage and splendid faith, Deborah was given supreme authority in Israel by the consent of the common people. This was an honor gained by no other woman mentioned in the Bible, a unique privilege that won for her the title, "Mother of Israel."

It was, however, during a period when her nation was menaced by war that Deborah rendered her greatest service to her country and won for herself lasting fame. Though she was well aware that the Israelites had incurred God's disfavor by their neglect and offenses, her faith in the Lord's help never wavered. She knew that the Lord would rescue His Chosen People, if only they would honor Him and return to His service.

Deborah summoned good military leadership and planned and succeeded in a campaign to destroy the oppressors of the Israelites. Through her great bravery, she conquered the Canaanite commander who had formidable military power at his disposal.

Deborah

Deborah exemplifies initiative, courage and resourcefulness in meeting challenging situations. As people in our modern society have greater opportunities to demonstrate these admirable qualities, women loyal to the Judeo-Christian tradition can be a powerful influence for good not only inside the home but outside as well, as in the workplace and by their active participation in the affairs of the community and in the democratic process.

15

DESTINED TO BE KING

David and Goliath

One day when the Israelites faced the army of their Philistine enemy, Goliath, a champion Philistine soldier of great size and strength, came forward. Goliath said to his opponents, "If an Israelite kills me, the Israelites will win. But if I defeat the Israelite you choose, we, the Philistines, will be declared the conquerors." Both sides agreed, and young David said, "I will go. The God who saved me before, will also keep me safe now." Then, hurling a stone with his sling, David hit Goliath on the forehead, and the giant Philistine fell dead. From then on David became a hero.

Later, as the Israelite king, David defeated the Philistines again and captured Jerusalem. He is best known for being the greatest king of Israel and a writer of the "Book of Psalms." It was from David's kingly family that Jesus, the Messiah, came.

It is an American trait to pull for the underdog, perhaps because America herself has had to fight great forces to protect her freedom. America has, from British imperialists to the reign of the demented fascist, Adolph Hitler, stared in the face of Goliath many a time but has relied on righteousness and the hand of God to aim her sling surely. Although as Americans we encounter great problems, we know that with God's help—only with God's help—we can overcome all obstacles in the way of truth and liberty.

David chosen king

WISER THAN ALL MEN

King Solomon

The splendor of the Temple he built in Jerusalem and the tales of his extraordinary wisdom overshadow the fact that Solomon's was a peaceful reign. Indeed the Hebrew root of his name, *shalom*, means peace. Throughout his reign of forty years, Solomon never led Israel into war. Solomon's message was that justice among men and peace among nations was pleasing to God.

Solomon became "wiser than all men," exceeding "all the children of the east, and all of the wisdom of Egypt," and many people came from near and far to engage in discussion with him.

Though he was young, Solomon was aware of the qualities indispensable to a leader. More than any other trait, he needed discernment: keen observation and accurate judgment. These are more vital than mere knowledge. Given this quality of mental clarity, a ruler may be just and fair and fulfill his responsibilities honorably; without it he is a despot, sowing destruction.

We should learn from Solomon, and require of our leaders the qualities he cultivated. All too often we can be taken in by a polished or cultivated image. But our nation yearns for leaders the caliber of Solomon, wise yet humble, and most loving of their Creator.

PROPHET AND STATESMAN

Isaiah the prophet was also a statesman of high quality. In him were united deep religious feeling and a profound knowledge of the world and everyday life.

Great in thought and action, Isaiah was stalwart in his religious demands upon the people and unhesitating in his political advice to the king. This unique mixture contradicts the common assumption that religion and life are incompatible—that to be religious is to live in an ivory tower apart from the real world.

Religion has a definite role in daily life, said Isaiah. But he admonished the people, "Bring no more vain oblations." It is useless merely to bring sacrifices to the Temple; ritual alone is no evidence that one is religious. When ceremony is coupled with just deeds and righteous behavior, however, the combination has meaning. "Seek justice, relieve the oppressed, judge the fatherless, plead for the widow." Isaiah was ready with suggestions for action that are appropriate in every age. As the early leaders of our nation knew, to help improve society is to act religiously.

Isaiah was a visionary, far ahead of his time, and of ours. His words still direct us toward the glories of the Messianic Age, when universal peace will reign, when nations "shall beat their swords into plowshares, and their spears into pruning hooks; nation shall not lift up sword against nation, neither shall they learn war any more."

There are those throughout the history of the United States who have carried their religious beliefs into the realm of civic action. American society was engendered by individuals who believed in standards of moral conduct to be lived in public as well as private life. Let us look to Isaiah's forthrightness as our own need for morally grounded civic activism becomes more and more apparent.

Isaiah

19

THE RINGING VOICE

Jeremiah was a prophet during one of the most difficult periods in the history of his people. Twice he saw his country overrun and his countrymen either killed or driven into exile.

Jeremiah saw that Babylon was swollen with victory when the Egyptian armies crumbled in its path, and he feared that Judah would be overrun as well. Desperately, he exhorted King Jehoiakim and the people to heed the danger and to abandon their indiscretions. He admonished them to strengthen their cities with the discipline taught in the Torah so that catastrophe might be averted. But he preached to heedless crowds. It seemed that only Baruch, his trusted secretary, listened as he recorded Jeremiah's sermons.

The Babylonian armies came, wreaking havoc in the land and destroying the Temple Solomon had built. The second Temple suffered a similar fate at the hands of the Romans. Annually, the date of the destruction of the Temple has been observed by the Jewish people as a day of mourning, as Jeremiah mourned the sins of his people.

Throughout his prophetic career, Jeremiah suffered much personal hardship. He was falsely accused of being a deserter. He was beaten, reviled, mocked, imprisoned, and cast into a pit. Nevertheless, regardless of the difficulties he had encountered, Jeremiah did not shirk his responsibility. His voice is still heard ringing with optimistic conviction: "For I am with thee to save thee and to deliver thee, saith the Lord."

In our land, we have seen many courageous individuals who suffered greatly for their convictions. Those who fought and died for democratic ideals must never be forgotten, just as those who became prisoners of war should stand forever as American heroes, deserving of our gratitude and homage. With the moral decay we see in modern society, let us look to individuals like Jeremiah, firm in their resolve to stand for standards of conduct that reflect the moral good.

Jeremiah and Baruch

IN THE DEN OF LIONS

Daniel was a lad of fifteen when he was taken into captivity in Babylon. Together with other youths chosen for their great ability, physical appearance, good moral character and high station, Daniel was given a thorough education in the culture of the conquerors. A brilliant student, he quickly learned the Chaldean language and the arts and sciences of his new environment. When the course of instruction, however, called for the abrogation of the teachings and practices of his faith, Daniel objected. He refused to give up praying to his God, even though it meant death in the lions' den.

As the Greek way of life invaded the countries of the Middle East, the people readily adopted the ways of Greek culture. Although the Jewish people did accept many Greek customs, they resented the decree that they no longer study the Torah or observe the Sabbath. They were horrified when their Temple was defiled. As a result, many took up arms in rebellion against this invasion of their religious life, and were joined by their countrymen.

The great body of people rallied in defense of the principle

Daniel

of religious freedom. The Jewish people were ready to sacrifice their lives for the right to worship God as they believed. They refused to surrender their faith in God and the discipline of their religion.

To fortify their flagging spirits, the story of Daniel was told. He became their hero because he spoke to the heart of their problem. Daniel had remained faithful to the teachings and practices of Judaism in the full face of danger, and God helped him overcome successfully the hazardous obstacles which were placed in his path. His display of loyalty encouraged the people to follow his brave example.

The dilemma of the Jewish people of this time is not unlike that which early immigrants to the New World faced. Religious freedom was paramount in the minds of the early settlers and indeed became, in the 18th century, an issue seen to require constitutional safeguards. Unfortunately, even with the First Amendment, modern society forces many courageous Americans to fight for the "free exercise" of their religion. With Judeo-Christian standards under such attack, Daniel still stands as a stalwart model of loyalty to one's moral principles and the right to live them out.

BEAUTIFUL AND BRAVE

Esther was a lovely maiden chosen by King Ahaseurus to become the Queen of Persia when Queen Vashti incurred his disfavor. Esther soon found herself in a crisis. The king did not know that Esther was a Jew because she remained silent about her background. When Haman, the king's grand vizier, requested permission to put to death all the Jewish people in his realm of 127 provinces, Esther was in a quandary.

As long as her faith was secret, Esther would have been safe in the palace. But she was brave as she was beautiful, and charming besides. She decided to intercede on behalf of her people, even if it meant her life.

To plead for her people, Esther planned to present herself before the king, unannounced, an offense that was punishable by death.

King Ahaseurus, seeing her in the doorway, was overwhelmed by Esther's radiant beauty. He overlooked her trespass and invited her into his throne room. This gave her the opportunity to plead for her people. Symbolically, as Esther was spared, so were the Jewish people, while the villainous Haman fell victim to his own plot.

Esther's story represents the eternal miracle of Jewish survival. The survival of our own nation has been no less due to the countless acts of bravery and generosity of spirit by unsung heroes and heroines.

As Americans, we can look to Esther's willingness to sacrifice herself for her people as a trait necessary for the survival of a great nation.

Queen Esther

A MAN OF GREAT FAITH

A man of wealth and goodness

Job was a man of virtue and piety, blessed by God with wealth and children. God pointed to Job as an example, but Satan cast doubt upon his virtue. After all, Job had great wealth; if he were poor, he would not be so pious. God accepted Satan's challenge: He would permit him to put Job to the test.

Thereupon, sudden and severe calamities swept away Job's wealth and took his children's lives. Submissively he bowed to the ordeal and his spiritual integrity held fast.

Having withstood the first test, Job was then put to a second one. Would he persevere in his devotion if he himself were afflicted? Confident of Job's faithfulness, God again turned him over to Satan, but instructed him to spare Job's life.

Smitten with tortuous boils, Job stubbornly maintained his faith in God. Satan lost his wager, but he enabled Job to portray the difference between the truly religious person and the superficially religious: how does he react to the adversity? Everyone must experience suffering; how he endures it reflects his faith. Job's response to poverty, death and sickness is a valuable lesson. Because these things occur is no reason to forego belief in the Almighty or faith in God's ever-present care. Job went even further and declared, "Though He slay me, yet will I trust in Him."

Many of America's citizens, from those who fled the Irish potato famine of the mid-19th century, to the African-Americans up from slavery, have had their faith put to the test through personal affliction, poverty, prejudice and oppression. The story of Job has also comforted countless individuals in the grips of disease and suffering. If we, as a nation, remain steadfast in our adherence to Judeo-Christian standards, then we can, and must, overcome the forces of poverty and racism and we can, and will, endure the suffering that comes our way.

Job with his friends

ANSWERING GOD'S CALL: THE STORY OF JESUS

The great events in the life of Jesus Christ at one time informed the conscience of America. From the Nativity story to the Resurrection our collective American sense of what is right and wrong was influenced greatly by the story of Jesus as He walked the earth in human form with His disciples and friends, and by His ever-instructive and salvific words. This sense of right and wrong, this precious notion of the sacred is slipping through our fingers in what some have called the post-Christian era. In our not so thoroughly modern desire to understand ourselves Christians tend to forget their greatest source of knowledge and personal fulfillment: the second person of the Holy Trinity, Jesus Christ.

What He did, what He said and, most of all, who He was and continues to be, has everything to do with how each of us as individual American citizens decides how to lead our lives. The person of Jesus Christ has everything to do with how we interact with our fellows, regardless of race, creed, color, or religion, in the foundation and maintenance of strong communities. And strong communities once were–and must again become–the cornerstone of our great nation.

Let us not only look to Jesus' human struggle to inform those around Him, but also to His God nature, for it is Jesus–true God and true Man–for whom the Christian calls "My Lord and Savior."

The Savior

MARY IS CHOSEN

The story of Our Lord Jesus Christ begins with a woman, for Our Lord was truly Man as well as God. The Virgin Mary was chosen from all time to have the greatest honor a creature could enjoy.

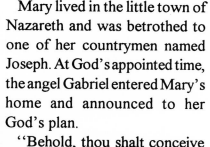

Mary lived in the little town of Nazareth and was betrothed to one of her countrymen named Joseph. At God's appointed time, the angel Gabriel entered Mary's home and announced to her God's plan.

"Behold, thou shalt conceive in thy womb and shalt bring forth a Son, and thou shalt call his name Jesus. He shall be great and shall be called Son of the Most High..." To Mary, familiar with the prophesies of the Savior, this could mean only one thing: she was to become the mother of Christ.

Showing extraordinary prudence in the face of such astonishing news, Mary requested further explanation, for she had never been with a man. In this wonderful girl there was not the slightest hint of prudery. The angel Gabriel, matching her frankness, then told her of the divine plan, which ensured that she would be the Anointed One, yet remain a Virgin.

Mary, like any other human being, was free to reject or comply with God's will. Her glorious reply will always ring in our grateful ears— "Behold the handmaiden of the Lord. Be it done unto me according to thy word."

Mary, the mother of Jesus

A PROPHETIC VISIT

The Angel Gabriel, in revealing to Mary the wondrous news that she was to be the Mother of Christ, had also told her that her cousin, Elizabeth, though advanced in years, would bear a son. This important link between the Savior and His herald, John the Baptist, was established even in the womb.

Setting out on the three days' journey, Mary hastened to her cousin's side. Entering the house of Elizabeth, Mary greeted her, and immediately the infant John leaped in the Elizabeth's womb. At that moment Mary's privilege was revealed to Elizabeth and she cried out with a loud voice: "Blessed art thou among women, and blessed is the fruit of thy womb. And whence is this to me, that the mother of my Lord should come to me?"

So that we may always be reminded of Mary's cooperation through her motherhood in the founding of Christ's Kingdom, the Scriptures tell us, "For, behold, from henceforth all generations shall call me blessed."

After a three month's stay with Elizabeth, Mary bade her farewell and returned home. She had much to attend to in preparation for the greatest birth of all time.

Elizabeth

THE NATIVITY

Shortly after Mary's return from her cousin's home, the simple marriage ceremony, conducted according to Jewish custom, was completed, and Joseph led his bride to his own home, where they began their married life, a model of dedication and simplicity.

The Roman Emperor, Augustus, issued an edict that all his subject peoples register in their city of origin. The family of Joseph originated in Bethlehem, so he was obliged to make the journey there from Nazareth. Though knowing her time was near at hand, Mary, with utter trust in God, set out with Joseph on this arduous journey.

The only shelter Joseph could find for his wife was a little stable, probably owned by the people who conducted the inn, where they had sought admission in vain. Here in this lowly manger, Mary brought forth the King of Kings. A cold, drafty stable became the center of the universe.

As Mary and Joseph, rapt in loving devotion, bent over the Child, an angel announced the great news to a group of shepherds nearby. A chorus of angels filled them with their song proclaiming glory to God in heaven and peace to men on earth. Full of faith, the shepherds hastened to the stable and adored the God-Child.

The surroundings of poverty and discomfort that God chose for the birth of His Son must surely carry for us all an important message. Consistently, Our Lord would teach, by word and example, the necessity of self-denial. So, from His first moment on earth, He would show us that though He might have chosen splendor and luxury, He chose a borrowed stable for His birth as, at death, He chose a borrowed grave.

Christ is born in Bethlehem

ADORATION OF THE MAGI

Since Christ was the King of Kings, it was suitable that He should have recognition from representatives of the pagan world. And so Providence decreed that the Wise Men (Magi), scholar-priests of the Gentile world, led by the star, should come to Bethlehem.

Following the star, the Magi proceeded to Jerusalem, confident of gathering there reliable information. Their simple question "Where is He that is born the King of the Jews?" created great excitement. King Herod, a tyrant, and detested by his people, became alarmed immediately, for he feared he would lose the throne. He called the Sanhedrin, the ecclesiastical council of the Jews, and asked them, "Where should Christ be born?" The prophecy was quite explicit on this point. The answer was "Bethlehem." Sending for the Magi, Herod gave them this information and cunningly told them to report back to him later, so that he too might adore the new King.

Eventually the Wise Men located the humble dwelling of the Holy Family. Oblivious to these humble surroundings, they prostrated themselves in homage. They then presented their gifts: gold, frankincense and myrrh—frankincense, for this Child is God; gold, for He is King of Kings; and myrrh, for He is man as well as God. After a short stay, the Wise Men warned by God of Herod's hypocrisy, disappeared as mysteriously as they had come.

And when they were come into the house, they saw the young Child with Mary his mother, and fell down, and worshipped Him...

Matthew 2:11

The Wise Men pay homage to the Christ Child.

THE
EARLY YEARS

The divine plan for Jesus was that as a child He should lead a hidden life. In Nazareth, Jesus quietly grew to maturity, to all appearances just another normal boy, obedient and respectful to his parents.

The Gospel reminds us, however, of His unique status by an episode from Jesus' 12th year. As pious Jews, Mary and Joseph made the annual pilgrimage to Jerusalem to celebrate the feast of the Pasch.

After the celebration, when the caravan was about to start on the return journey, Mary and Joseph discovered that Jesus was missing. They inquired anxiously about Him, thinking He might be with relatives and friends. But there was no sign of Him. They decided to return to Jerusalem to search for Him. At last, on the third day, they found Him in the Temple, astounding the doctors with His wisdom. Before Him sat the venerable rabbis as this young Boy so masterfully took charge of the discussion. Such discussion was common; but a boy of twelve, questioning and answering with such wisdom was indeed unique. Jesus expounded the Scriptures with a startling clarity.

Perplexed by the whole incident, His mother asked for an explanation. Jesus simply reminded her that He was performing a task assigned Him by His Father in heaven.

Jesus then obediently returned with them to Nazareth where, for the next eighteen years, He was subject to them.

The carpenter shop

Jesus with John the Baptist

THE COMING OF
JOHN THE BAPTIST

The promise of the Savior was the cornerstone of Jewish culture, their support in the midst of all the trials and tribulations witnessed by their race. Again and again their prophets had foretold it. They knew the prophecies telling of the herald who would come before the King, preparing His way. "The voice of one crying in the wilderness. Prepare ye the way of the Lord."

John the Baptist was well-known to many. His father was a prominent man, and the circumstances of John's birth were still remembered. His life as a hermit was in itself a fascination to people. Now he had emerged from his solitude and preached the coming of Christ, in fulfillment of his role as herald. The Jewish spiritual leaders had always been particular about their dress and in their attention to the letter of the law. John the Baptist clothed himself with whatever came readily to hand—a garment of camel's hair, for instance. In his preaching, he broke through the details of the Law and sought to reach the very hearts of men.

After the harvest season, we find Jesus emerging from His hidden life. The news of John's preaching had reached Galilee, and a group set out to hear him. One member of this group was Jesus, the carpenter. At the Jordan, He and the others stopped to listen. Unassuming as ever, Jesus stepped forward to be baptized, last of the group. John did not know at first who He was, so perfect was Jesus' humility. Yet, even before God revealed it to him, he knew that this Man should be the one baptizing. This was the One for whom John was herald. Our Lord, however, meek and submissive, overcame his protests and insisted on being baptized.

Showing submission on his part, John obeyed. After the baptism, when Jesus stepped from the water, the Holy Spirit descended on Him in the form of a dove, and a voice from heaven said, "This is my beloved Son in whom I am well pleased."

The Temptation of Christ

THE PUBLIC LIFE BEGINS

After His baptism, Jesus went to a desert region and remained there fasting and praying for forty days, preparing for his public life. Satan, aware of approaching salvation through Christ, used every weapon in his armory to stave off failure. Jesus answered his temptations with a declaration of war, and sent him scurrying off to defeat.

Soon disciples began to seek Jesus, calling Him "Rabbi," indicating that they had accepted Him as their Master: first Andrew, then his brother Simon (to be called Peter), then Philip, and later, the rest of the Twelve.

All was now ready, and the Master would go forth to teach. Now He would work miracles that His people might believe in Him. He chose as the scene of His first public miracle a wedding feast at Cana, where in answer to His mother's request

Christ's first miracle

He changed water into wine.

A year had passed and Christ continued to preach and baptize.

His followers had grown in number, but Herod had thrown John the Baptist into jail, and Judeans had shown poor response to Jesus' teachings.

One day, traveling through Samaria with His disciples, Jesus stopped by a well to rest. His own people regarded the Samaritans as heretics, and a bitter rivalry had grown up between them. A Samaritan woman came to the well to draw water. Convention forbade His talking to her, but He asked her for a drink and conversed with her. Soon, through His gentle guidance, she believed He was the Savior.

Jesus teaches love of God and love of neighbor.

SERMON ON THE MOUNT

After His two days in Samaria, Our Lord set out for His home town of Nazareth. On the way, He passed through Cana where He cured the ruler's son. In Nazareth, He sadly discovered that His townsmen, accusing Him of blasphemy, sought only to destroy Him. He escaped, however, to Capernaum (Capharnaum) where He settled and worked many miracles. In this town, He proved His claim of having the power to forgive sins by curing the paralytic. Soon the crippled and diseased flocked around Him, exhausting Him with their endless entreaties.

In His Manhood, He needed rest. So, embarking on a small boat at Bethsaida, He and the disciples sought peace and quiet on the lake. But there could be no rest, for much had to be done, and His work was only beginning.

The crowds returned, and there, on the hillside rising from the lake, Jesus preached the Sermon on the Mount. In this sermon, He gave the Apostles and the assembled people the great principles of His teaching—love of God, and love of neighbor.

The Golden Rule teaches us that our love for others must be based upon our love for God.

RETURNING TO CAPERNAUM

*"Wherefore
I say unto thee,
her sins,
which are many,
are forgiven;
for she loved
much..."*

Luke 7: 47

Mary Magdalene

On the return journey to Capernaum from the Mount, in the fashionable town of Magdala, Jesus again showed His love for those, who, though sinners, have a generous and loving heart. Invited to the house of Simon the Pharisee, He was treated to a cold politeness so often extended to their guests by the snobbish rich. Suddenly a woman ran into the dining hall and, in tears, prostrated herself before Jesus. With her hair, she wiped His feet, and poured perfumed ointment over them. She was a notorious sinner whom no "respectable" person would allow near.

Love is best expressed in deeds, and Christ called attention to His treatment by this woman compared to the frigid hospitality He had been receiving. Turning to the shocked onlookers, He told them that her many sins were forgiven because of her great love.

37

THE MIRACLES CONTINUE

As was His practice, when exhausted by His labors, Our Lord sought a few hours peace on the lake. This lake, or sea, of Galilee is about fourteen miles long and six miles across at its broadest part. Suddenly a freak wind hit the small craft, threatening to capsize it. Jesus lay asleep, untroubled. His Apostles panicked. They wakened Him, and He immediately quelled the storm. Then He chided them for their poor faith, reminding them that they needed, before all else, a strong faith in the Master.

Next morning, they put in at Gerasa and, scarcely rested, recrossed the lake and returned to Jesus' beloved Capernaum. More miracles were to come. He cured the woman with the issue of blood and raised the daughter of Jairus to life. Now Jesus' fame spread throughout the countryside; nevertheless, when He returned to Nazareth, He found His townsmen still rejected Him.

Jesus calms the storm

"*...when the people were put forth, He went in, and took her by the hand, and the maid arose.*"

Matthew 9: 25

Jesus heals the daughter of Jairus.

Soon the Twelve returned from preaching in the cities, enthusiastic in their accounts of their work. But once more the crowds pressed; and to escape them, they took a ship to a desert place to rest. But the crowds followed the sail to meet Jesus where He landed. Touched by this devotion, He came ashore and taught them. Here He worked the miracle of the loaves and fishes. Thwarting their efforts to make Him king, Our Lord bade the Apostles to take ship for Bethsaida, while He dismissed the people. That night, again showing the Apostles the importance of faith, He came walking over the water to join them as they sailed.

THE RAISING OF LAZARUS

Martha

Jesus cherished the close friendship He had with Lazarus and his two sisters, Martha and Mary, and He often visited them at their home in Bethany. Lazarus had become gravely ill, but no one knew better than his sisters of the healing powers of Jesus.

They sent a message to Him saying simply, "He whom Thou lovest is sick." When He got the news, Jesus observed that everything would turn out all right and that the whole incident would provide an occasion for further glory to God.

The disciples were pleased at this reaction. They were, at the moment, working quietly in Perea and the Master was prudent in not risking any foolhardy trip into Judea. Suddenly however, He told them to get ready to go to Bethany, for Lazarus, their friend, was dead.

As Jesus and the Twelve approached the house, so well-known to all of them, Martha, the practical one, came running to meet them. She told Jesus that Lazarus would not have died had He been there; but, more important, since anything He asks of God will be granted, her brother can be raised to life again if Jesus so wills. Then Mary, hearing of His arrival, ran to Him and characteristically threw herself at His feet, pouring out her grief. Profoundly touched, Jesus Himself wept, but only momentarily for His teaching was of joy and hope.

They made their way to the tomb, and Jesus began to pray to His Father. In a loud voice He said, "Lazarus, come forth!" All about the sepulcher were entranced. Lazarus came walking out of the tomb, bound in the death shroud. Jesus then made His way to the house, later to be joined by the family in a grateful reunion. He left the crowds with their wonder—a man dead and buried four days had been raised to life.

Mary of Bethany

"Lazarus, come forth!"

THE LAST SUPPER

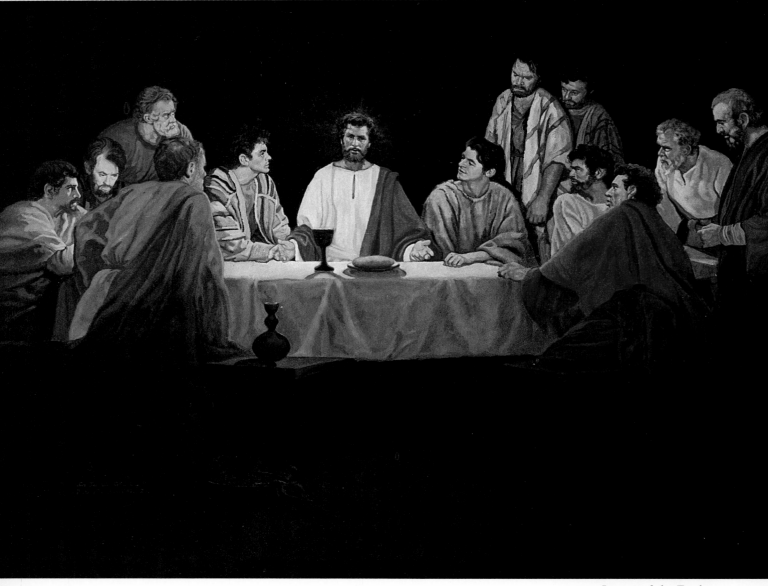

Jesus and the Twelve

The Sanhedrin, a council composed of chief priests, scribes and elders, having now finally rejected Jesus, met one night in the house of Caiaphas. Christ's popularity made them plot to take Him secretly. Thus did Judas, the traitor, play into their hands by his offer to betray Jesus. They agreed to pay him thirty shekels, about seventeen dollars, for his treachery.

On a Thursday morning, the day of the Pasch, Jesus sent Peter and John to Jerusalem to find a room and prepare for the paschal meal, where He, with the others, joined them in the evening. Before the supper, the Master set them an example of humility by washing the feet of each. When the meal was over, Jesus told them that He knew one of them would betray Him. Stunned, each one blurted out, "Is it I, Lord?" Judas, sitting near, asked the same question. Our Lord replied quietly, "Thou has said it." Rejecting Jesus' offer of repentance, Judas hurried out into the night.

Then Jesus fulfilled His promise to give His flesh and blood as our food and drink. He blessed and broke bread and giving it to them bade them eat it saying, "This is My body." Then He took the cup and giving thanks gave it to them with the words, "Drink ye all of this. For this is My blood of the New Testament which is shed for many for the remission of sins." In these words, Jesus linked forever the ceremony of the Last Supper with His glorious Sacrifice on Calvary.

"...verily, verily, I say unto you, that one of you shall betray Me."

John 13:21

Judas Iscariot

CHRIST'S DESTINY APPROACHES

After these things, Jesus, as He conversed with them, predicted Peter's denial. He then consoled them in their shock and sorrow over what was to come. After leaving the supper room, they set out for Mount Olivet. Coming to Gethsemane, Jesus led the party to an olive grove. He took Peter, James and John with Him, away from the others. Though desiring their comforting presence, He withdrew to pray alone. Horrified in His human nature at the picture of His coming sufferings, a mixture of sorrow, fright, disgust and frustration flooded His soul. He cried out to His Father for relief but immediately qualified His prayer with submission, "Thy will be done."

During this phase an angel appeared to strengthen Him. Yet even with this help, so intense was the agony that blood oozed forth from the pores of His body, and trickled to the ground. Returning to seek solace from Peter, James and John, He found them asleep. Sadly, He chided them, and went back to His prayer and agony. Later, He returned and again found them asleep. Without a word, He went back to face the third, and last, phase of His agony.

The Agony in the Garden

THE ARREST,
AND PETER'S DENIAL

Calm and courageous once more after His prayer in Gethsemane, Jesus heard the approach of those who came to arrest Him, and told the Apostles that His hour was at hand. The rabble was made up of some members of the Sanhedrin with their servants and a number of Roman soldiers.

Judas led them toward Jesus and, in utter duplicity, greeted Him warmly. Turning from the traitor, He made it clear that He would deliver Himself to them. He allowed them to take Him, and they bound Him roughly. Inflamed at this rough handling, Peter, fiery as ever, took out a sword and slashed at one of Jesus' captors, injuring his right ear. Jesus restrained the Apostles, cautioning them against violence, and healed the injury. He was then dragged off to face the farce they referred to as a trial. After Our Lord's arrest, the Apostles had fled; but Peter, ashamed of his fear, soon returned and followed a short distance behind Christ's captors. Inside Caiaphas' palace, Peter was asked if he were not one of Christ's disciples. He replied, "I am not." Then he joined other servants warming themselves

Peter denies knowing Jesus.

around a fire in the courtyard, where a maidservant told him that he looked like one of the Twelve. Indignantly, Peter denied it—he denied even knowing Jesus. An hour later, some servants told him they were sure he was a follower of Jesus; his very speech gave him away. Peter swore vehemently

that he did not know Jesus.

During these denials, the unmistakable crowing of a cock was heard three times. Later, as Jesus was led from the palace, He fixed on Peter a searching look. His heart crushed, Peter fled from the palace and burst into bitter tears.

CHRIST BEFORE PILATE

At Caiaphas' palace, the sham continued, with false witnesses adding to the mockery. Jesus, calm throughout, announced that He was the Son of God. That was all that Caiaphas wanted. He obtained from the servile assembly a unanimous vote for the death sentence. Immediately, those who guarded Jesus struck Him and spat in His face. He endured all with heroic patience.

Pilate was impressed by the dignified bearing of Christ. So he returned Him to the Sanhedrin, and said he saw no reason for their accusations. Pilate's reply set off a clamor, and, hoping to evade responsibility, he told them to take Jesus to Herod Antipas, King of Galilee, since the accused was a Galilean. Herod simply used this directive as an occasion for mockery. Jesus was dressed in a white robe and was treated like a fool to entertain the court. Then Jesus was returned to Pilate.

The Governor, once more saddled with the responsibility of a decision, told the growing crowd outside his residence that he would punish Christ and release Him, for He did not deserve to die. Then a thought occurred to him—in deference to Jewish custom, the Romans released a prisoner during the paschal festival. So he offered the mob a choice between Barabbas, a murderer, and Jesus. This, Pilate thought, was the way out. But the mob's choice was definite and persistent; it wanted Christ crucified. Pilate thereupon turned Jesus over to his soldiers to be scourged.

Jesus announces He is the Son of God.

CHRIST IS CRUCIFIED

The Crucifixion

rucify Him, crucify Him," was the persistent scream from the mob, as Pilate presented Jesus to them. Though convinced of His innocence, the spineless Pilate pandered to the mob and pronounced the condemnation: "Thou shalt go on the cross." As was the custom, the execution of the sentence would take place immediately. The procession was formed, a centurion leading the way, next a herald, announcing the reason for the condemnation, then Jesus, bent over, with the heavy cross upon His back.

The hill of Calvary was about a thousand yards from Pilate's residence and, fearing Jesus would collapse from exhaustion before getting there, the soldiers seized a man named Simon the Cyrenian and forced him to carry the cross. On the way, a group of women, overcome by sorrow, publicly sobbed as Jesus passed by. Touched by their hearts, He turned to them and softly, in a voice blurred with weakness, told them to keep their grief for themselves and their children, referring to the dreadful destruction that would descend upon Jerusalem.

When Calvary had been reached, Jesus was offered, in accordance with ancient custom, a stimulant concocted of wine and myrrh. This small concession He barely touched with His bruised and parched lips. His bloodstained garments were ripped away; His hands nailed to the transverse bar of the Cross. Then they nailed His feet. He did not scream as they drove in the nails. His only words were, "Father, forgive them, for they know not what they do."

The extreme of physical agony was not His only suffering. He had to witness the utter misery of His mother as the sword, foretold by Simeon, pierced her heart.

On all sides, a somber curtain of agony misted His eyes. Jesus was dying.

"Father, into Thy hands I commend My spirit!"

JESUS DIES ON THE CROSS

As Jesus hung on the cross, the soldiers, as was their grisly right according to law, cast lots for His garments, unwittingly fulfilling the prophesy of the twenty-second Psalm which foretells the parting of Jesus' garments and the casting of lots on His vesture. The two brigands crucified on either side of Christ, mingled their mockery with that of the others. They reminded Him of His claim of being able to rebuild the Temple in three days--of His saving others, and contemptuously told Him He now could not save Himself.

Suddenly, however, one of them, realizing the heinousness of it all, turned to Christ, and contritely asked Him to remember him when He shall come as King. The dying Jesus, returning kindness for insult, gently replied, "This day thou shalt be with me in Paradise."

Ever a loving Son, Our Lord's thoughts were with His mother. Each pang of grief she suffered He shared with her. Solicitous for her well-being, He committed her to the care of His beloved disciple, John.

About noon, the heavens marked their disapproval and cast over the dreadful scene a curtain of gloom, which continued until three o'clock. Shortly before that fatal hour, Jesus' entire human nature rose in final distress, as cruelty heaped upon cruelty, and a cry of utter agony escaped from His lips, "My God, my God, why hast Thou forsaken Me?" No words could better portray the extremity of His suffering.

Burning with fever, He gasped, "I thirst," and a bystander took a sponge, dipped in a mixture of vinegar and water and, fastening it to a branch of hyssop, held it up to Jesus' mouth. His lips thus moistened, He indicated that His work on earth had been accomplished and that He was now ready to die. Quoting the Psalms, He uttered His last words, teeming with love of His Father until the end. "Father, into Thy hands I commend My spirit!" Then, with a final cry of pain, His outraged humanity reached the limit of endurance, and Jesus Christ, on the altar of the cross, bowed His head and died.

Jesus rises from the dead.

AN EMPTY TOMB

The Mosaic Law stipulated that a corpse, after execution, not be left overnight; so the Sanhedrin, ever observant of the letter of the Law, petitioned Pilate to issue a command that the legs of those who hung on the cross be broken to hasten their death. The soldiers who came to carry out this order found Jesus already dead. One of them, however, to make sure, drove his spear into Jesus' right side, and from the gaping wound there streamed a mixture of blood and water.

Before anything further could be done with the Sacred Body, Joseph of Arimathæa, loyal to Jesus though a member of the Sanhedrin, used his influence to obtain Pilate's permission to take charge of the dead Christ. Joseph took the body from the cross, and Jesus' mother, with others, washed the body and wrapped it in bandages sprinkled with aromatic spices, and covered it with a shroud provided by Joseph of Arimathæa, who also offered a tomb, located only a few yards from Calvary. Then the small funeral procession—Mary, the holy women, and a few disciples—took the body to the sepulcher and Jesus was buried.

Next day, the Sabbath, all was quiet. Early on the following morning a group of women, led by Mary Magdalene, went to the tomb to find someone to help them roll back the stone, for they wanted to attend further care on Jesus' body. On their arrival, they found the stone rolled back and the soldiers lying terrified on the ground. Astonished, they were told by an angel that Jesus had risen, as He said He would, and they were to go and tell Peter and the others that the Master had gone into Galilee. Mary Magdalene, however, as soon as she had seen the open door of the tomb, surmised that someone had taken the body. Immediately, she fled to bear word to Peter and John. On receiving this news, they hurried to the sepulcher. Peter entered first, and saw the bandages and shroud carefully folded and laid aside. Then John came in and looked around the empty tomb; in the words of the Scripture, "He saw and believed."

The Ascension

JESUS ASCENDS INTO HEAVEN

Shortly after Christ had risen from the dead, He appeared to Mary Magdalene. At first she thought He was the gardener and, overcome with grief, pleaded with him to tell her where her Master's body had been taken. Then Jesus spoke one word, "Mary." It was enough. She threw herself at His feet crying out, "Master!"

On Sunday afternoon two disciples were on their way from Jerusalem to the village of Emmaus. As they walked along discussing the distressing events of the last few days, Jesus joined them. But they did not recognize Him. When they reached Emmaus, Jesus accepted their invitation to join them in a meal. Breaking bread, He handed a piece to each. As soon as He had done so, the disciples realized that their companion was Jesus; but, before they could say a word, the Master disappeared.

As the two disciples, who had returned from Emmaus and joined the others at Jerusalem, excitedly recounted their experience, Jesus joined the group and showed them the wounds in His hands and feet.

Later the Apostles left Jerusalem and went to Galilee. One evening, Peter, with six other Apostles, set out to fish on the lake. All night they fished, but caught nothing. At dawn they saw a stranger on the shore; when they had pulled near, this man told them to cast their net on the other side of the boat. They did so, and immediately made such a catch that they could not raise the net. At once Peter recognized Him and, crying out to the others, "It is the Lord," jumped into the water with his usual impetuosity, and swam the hundred yards to the shore.

In a happy reunion, they built a little fire, made a meal at His invitation and then settled down to hear the Master's words. He took this occasion to continue their training for the commission He had given them to "teach all nations, baptizing them in the name of the Father, and of the Son, and of the Holy Ghost." This training the Holy Spirit would complete on Pentecost.

At the appointed time, Our Lord's devoted followers went to Jerusalem and were met by the Master, who imparted to them His final instruction. His last words uttered, Jesus Christ, true God and true man, whose birth was a miracle, left the earth also in miraculous fashion. With His mother, the Apostles, disciples, and holy women gathered around Him on Mount Olivet, He bade them farewell and, as He blessed them, rose in great majesty until a cloud hid Him from sight.

OUR AMERICAN HERITAGE

DEFINING LIBERTY:
THE AMERICAN WAY OF LIFE

A Grand Experiment

For about six thousand years, man has left written records of the profound events that have affected him. It was at the beginning of that period that civilizations were growing up not far from the land bridge which is Palestine. Later these civilizing forces swept on to the West, first through Europe and then across the ocean with the earliest settlers. Here in this country, we have added our own contribution. We call it the *American Way of Life*, perhaps the best expression of what God intended we should strive for.

Surely human dignity has risen to greater heights for greater numbers in America than in any other country. In a little over three centuries man brought to finer fruition on these shores more real progress than the fifty-seven previous centuries had yielded anywhere else on earth. That is indeed a remarkable accomplishment and forms a proud heritage.

It seems to us as though a beneficent God has set apart this land so that a grand experiment might here be carried through to a successful fulfillment.

That experiment seeks to prove two very fundamental principles. The first principle is that individual human energy and creativity flow most abundantly when generated by individuals in their own *self-interest* and that individuals *alone* can best control the energy and creativity they generate. The companion truth is that where there is a conflict of rights, the further pursuit of our activities would no longer truly be in our self-interest. Self-

interest will continue to rule in such situations; and we soon learn to join with others for common purposes beyond our capacity as individuals.

This is a grand break with the form of governmental authority which pagan philosophies had established and maintained since the beginning of recorded history.

The notion is that we are *free*, only so long as we are able to determine our own destinies. When we are our own masters, and employ our efforts under the drive of self-interest, we go farther and faster, and with greater security to all concerned.

The colonists learned these deep truths quickly by first-hand experience. They made most certain progress when their efforts were untrammeled by man-made restrictions. They had shucked off the hampering restraints which they had known in the Old World at the hands of monarchical governments. And when these governments tried to transplant such handicaps into this country through royally appointed governors, the colonists were incensed; and in some cases resorted to arms to contest their rights.

Finally there came a showdown in the matter of the right of the English Parliament to regiment them in the ''public interest.'' The Revolutionary War was the result; and the freedom thus bought was to be cherished and perpetuated. The colonists' experience with government restrictions had been such that when they were forced to set up some common authority for the thirteen colonies—now states—it was, at first, so weak as to be practically worthless. They much preferred to err on the side of prudence.

Even when the time came to strengthen this central government so that there might be a "more perfect union," Thomas Jefferson expressed the caution common to all when he said, "I own I am not a friend of the energetic government. *It is always oppressive.*"

Thus it was the sincere hope of the framers of the Constitution that what they provided would be not only a government of law, rather than of men, but also that it would be constituted in such a way that it would not become a heavy yoke about the necks of the governed.

The consequence was an authority most carefully thought out, and planned with the chief purpose of making freedom real and inalienable. The federal government—all government—was to be small in numbers and, by today's standards, in power. Still it was sufficiently adequate to meet and overcome every situation with which it was confronted.

Actually it was not until near the end of the last century that this original idea began to change, and then but slowly. Even during the early years of the present century our federal administrative body increased in numbers and in stature at a fairly moderate pace.

We must never forget, however, what the American Experiment, carried out on this continent, proved. Only the individual can expand energy and creativity to the greatest possible benefit. Of late we have tended to lay these truths on the shelf, and let a new pattern of thinking creep into our scheme of government. The trend is characterized by a dangerously abundant regimentation of our lives.

Of course, the dictates of Natural Law and reason provide that certain moral tenets demand complete acquiescence. No one should be free to take the life of an innocent human being or to ignore another's claim to personal property through thievery or embezzlement. To claim such freedom is unspeakable aberrance. And while we are willing, however, to surrender certain other *legitimate* liberties as a matter of self-interest and for the good of the whole, we must be careful not to unwittingly relinquish our great heritage of freedom. Further regimentation prepares the way for greater seizure of rights by government. Our forefathers energetically resisted such regimentation.

Contemporary Problems

A number of contemporary cultural trends can, if not employed wisely, affect the democratic process in a negative way.

Pressures exerted by special interest groups or professional lobbyists, for instance, should always be examined critically. The right of protest is inherent in the *American Way of Life*, and nothing tending to bar it should be permitted. But before giving allegiance to any group, it is prudent to be certain that the group's philosophy is in keeping with what we believe to be the best for our country and for our children.

Modern communications technology can condition us to believe that information, in and of itself, is morally good, and therefore true. Data may indeed be used as a moral means to a moral end, or it may be used in high-tech schemes of deception, or to lull us into amoral subjectivism, where any idea is as inherently good as any other idea regardless of the possible consequences of its application. This matter of conditioning is critical. It applies to the individual and to our political culture in general.

Because of communication technology, and a more mobile population, national thinking can now be influenced more effectively than ever before. We are today subjected to a constant barrage of propaganda such as no generation before us ever had to withstand. And the government has adapted many techniques made effective in the fields of advertising, promotion and public relations.

By such means, different interpretations are being given to some of the older American attitudes from which we have drawn strength in the past. Belief in individual initiative has been watered down. Self-reliance has been too extensively replaced by reliance upon government. And even our respect for age-old virtues and morality is being called into question.

Another of our contemporary problems is complacency. No previous generation has had its passions so continuously exercised. Movies and videos, television and radio, and other media play continually upon our emotions, until we become emotionally passive. Where citizens used to raise their voices and pound their fists in the discussion of current affairs, today there is little more than a shrug of the shoulders. Can it be that we no longer value liberty as we once did?

There was a self-appointed disciple of ''downtrodden'' peoples in the 19th century named Karl Marx. The doctrine he preached is known to us today as *communism*. What he proposed was to *take* ''from each according to his abilities,'' and then to *give* ''to each according to his needs.''

Read quickly and without thinking out all that it implies, this formula seemed almost inspired. Marx was so certain of wide acceptance that he predicted every nation in the world would make his proposal the pattern of government.

Of course, the events of recent history have revealed that Marx's errant socialistic philosophy ultimately translates into severe oppression of the human spirit. As a philosophical system, it devalues individual liberty and, as an economic system, it fails to cultivate, and therefore benefit from, the ingenuity of citizens working in their own self-interests. And a citizenry long stifled will, inevitably, as in the former Soviet Union and surrounding lands, break their shackles and demand a system of governance more akin to democratic ideals—ideals grounded in individual liberty and, therefore, individual moral responsibility.

Some have been conditioned to think of government as being solely *for* the people. We do well to review Lincoln's Gettysburg Address, where he outlined a ''government *of* the people,'' and then ''*by* the people,'' since it is only in that way that it can be a government ''*for* the people.''

Mistaken emphasis on government being *for* us can be dangerous thinking. Such a philosophy nearly wrecked Jamestown in 1607 and Plymouth in 1620. What reason is there to believe it will not have equally baneful results today?

The Need for Moral Resolve

As the embarrassed Jefferson sat and heard the Declaration which he had drafted debated word by word by the Continental Congress, he no doubt subscribed readily to two changes which were made. They occur in the last, and in the next to last sentences. In the latter instance, the assembly inserted the clause ''appealing to the Supreme Judge of the world for the rectitude of our intentions.'' They went on record to show their willingness to submit their acts to the Father above to be judged.

In the last sentence they frankly sought His guidance and support, as indicated by the inclusion of ''with firm reliance upon the Protection of Divine Providence.''

These early legislators wished their acts not only to be legally sound but morally honest as well.

Can it be that our anxiety today really stems not so much from economic conditions as from weakened —and no more than lukewarm— morality? The early Puritans erred in the direction of religious excess, but the moral basis they and other settlers gave to Colonial times, and which was carried over into a young nation, was something to build upon.

Every public servant required to take the oath of allegiance when entering office completes it with the words, ''so help me God.'' Divine help was never more needed than today. Especially is such guidance needed in high places.

Although a former Justice of the Supreme Court contended that there are no longer any ''absolutes,'' can that possibly be the prevailing feeling? Have the Ten Commandments no longer any standing at the bar of public opinion? Are there situations today where stealing, murder, adultery, or unbridled greed are to be condoned? What have become of our standards? Or have we none, other than for personal advantage —"what's in it for me?"

Our moral laws should be as fixed as the stars in the sky, as little subject to repeal as the laws of gravity. Otherwise the *American Way of Life* has moved off its solid-rock foundation and onto a bed of quicksand.

Our first impulse is to believe that yesterday was all moral rectitude, and what we need is a return to the "good old days." But it would be rank fallacy for us to think that human nature had altered greatly—and for the worse—in recent years. Conditions about us change, but man continues to be swayed by much the same impulses with which he was beset more than 3,400 years ago when the Ten Commandments were written out for his guidance on tablets of stone by the finger of God.

We do well to face the fact that there have been periods in our past when corruption has clouded our national life, both within, and without, the government.

An Ever-Better America

Yet lest we waver in our resolve, it should be realized that we have made substantial progress in numerous aspects of government and business practices since the turn of the century.

"Unless the Lord build the house, they labor in vain that build it," said the psalmist. It was true more than two thousand years ago when these words were penned; our forefathers knew it to be true, and it must be our guide today. Without attention to the objective standards of the Judeo-Christian tradition, our founders' dream of liberty may vanish. Our hope is clearly, as always, for an ever-better America.

We need to be vigilant in our watch against false prophets and their aberrant, subjective standards of morality.

We must also remember that Freedom can be *voted away* just as surely as it can be torn from us by violence.

Leaders who promise us *something for nothing* should be shunned like the plague. We must keep ever before us the fact that a government produces *nothing*. When a government *gives* it must first *take* from someone—and that someone is pretty certain to be *you and me*.

One privilege that is still ours and largely unimpaired is our *right* to vote. But when thirty, forty, even fifty percent of us refuse to exercise our right to state our preference for a candidate or for a cause, our American heritage seems to be in serious jeopardy.

Many, even in very recent history, have given their lives so that the democratic ideal of liberty, based upon standards of moral good passed to us from the Judeo-Christian tradition, could flourish unrestrained by tyranny in any form. As we are challenged by the codes of conduct inherent in these standards and as we cultivate them in the free exercise of religion, let us look to the basic units of social integration for strength.

The first place individual liberty can take hold is in the family. And although of late we have been forced to re-define the family unit as it functions in modern society, still the basic objective values, the proper and natural notions of what is right and what is wrong, must emanate from the family. If we continue to allow the family to disintegrate, our objective moral standards, the lifeline of our children, will evaporate.

Strong families form strong communities. And it is within the community that the individual pursues fulfillment through energetic and creative self-interest which, in turn, contributes to the well-being of the other individuals in the community.

Just as our forebears accepted these challenges, so a similar obligation rests upon us. It will be by our individual efforts and continuing staunch support that America will ever be a "Sweet Land of Liberty." Let us set our minds and hearts to work.

A REPUBLIC IS BORN

Upon signing the Declaration of Independence, Samuel Adams said, "We have this day restored the Sovereign to Whom all men ought to be obedient, and from the rising to the setting of the sun, let His Kingdom come." That the hand of Providence was guiding this great and noble experiment, which began as the colonies threw off the shackles of imperial Britain, is attested to again and again in the writings of the Founding Fathers. Their ideas on life, liberty and the pursuit of happiness were framed by a sense of humility which emanates from the Judeo-Christian bent of mind. That their God watched over them would be undenied in their ranks. They knew where their rights came from. As their great declaration proclaimed:

When in the course of human events, it becomes necessary for one people to dissolve the political bonds, which have connected them to another, and to assume among the powers of the earth, the separate and equal station to which the laws of Nature and of Nature's God entitle them, a decent respect to the opinions of mankind requires that they should declare the causes which compel them to the separation.

In so much as "Nature's God" guided them, the founders of this new nation were not wax figures or the stoic gazers of their painted portraits, but living, breathing people of passion, honorable but human, able to walk among the aristocracy of early America, but at home in the backwoods or, like a young, burly Washington, surveying a wilderness acreage, promising to himself that he would never stop sleeping out in the open air. They were learned but not in an isolated, merely academic sense. They, like Jefferson, took their restless ideas and applied them to a practical notion of governance based upon individual freedom and responsibility. As Abraham of old, their obedience to principles is what made them leaders. And like Moses, they loved the people they had found themselves serving.

Let us look briefly, but with reverence to our collective American past; a past that engendered modern democracy and demonstrated to us in its human representatives the divine sanctity of individual liberty.

"...their obedience to principles is what made them leaders."

The Second Continental Congress

The First Continental Congress had adjourned in the late spring of 1775 with but a few radicals calling for a break with Britain. But with the battles of Lexington and Concord, radical voices were buttressed in the Second Continental Congress meeting in Philadelphia. To stand in opposition to the British, a continental army was formed and through the influence of John Adams, a brawny but modest George Washington, at 43 years of age, was appointed commander-in-chief.

It would be just over a year later when Congress would adopt the Declaration of Independence. Although the Congress created political obstacles for Washington as commander and after the war declined in quality, as demonstrated by its eventual dissolution, still its early organization was essential to the founding of our nation.

Thomas Jefferson
1743-1826

One of the most influential American statesmen, Thomas Jefferson perhaps best exemplifies the moniker "Founding Father." Aside from slight alterations by John Adams, Benjamin Franklin and other congressional delegates the Declaration of Independence is primarily the work of Jefferson. His service to the new republic was most comprehensive. In 1779 he became governor of Virginia and served during the most difficult years of the American revolution. He served two terms as Virginia delegate to the Continental Congress. In 1789 he was appointed minister to France, succeeding Benjamin Franklin. He became Secretary of State in 1790. Jefferson was elected Vice President in 1796 and President for two terms beginning in 1800.

Jefferson believed in the efficacy of local government and local administration of that government's policies, leaving the federal government to concentrate mostly on foreign affairs. His political philosophy was challenged fiercely by Alexander Hamilton among others. Even after his retirement to Monticello however, Jefferson was called upon by succeeding Presidents James Madison and James Monroe for consultation. He was highly instrumental in the founding of the University of

Virginia and was President of the American Philosophical Society from 1797 to 1815.

There was no area of human intellectual achievement that did not interest Thomas Jefferson. Philosophy, literature, art, architecture, science and, of course, governance, all were passions of the learned statesman. And perhaps our country has never seen a more dedicated and articulate advocate of political and religious freedom than our third president. His constant defense of democratic principles in the face of early Federalist trends (which he thought to be dangerously close to a return to monarchical ideals) makes one wonder what direction our nation may have taken if not for adamant democratic-republicans like Thomas Jefferson, who lived their lives in service to a fledgling nation based upon Judeo-Christian principles of freedom and individual dignity and liberty.

"The Wisest American"

This is what Benjamin Franklin, 1706-1790, printer, scientist, inventor, writer, editor, philosopher, diplomat and statesman is sometimes called. He has become a beloved figure in our history not only for his insistence upon discipline, thrift, and other personal virtues, but for his patriotism and loyalty as the nation came into being.

With the same earnestness as in his early ventures into science and letters, Ben Franklin, in his later years, became more and more involved in the duties attendant to the American Revolution. He was a delegate to the Continental Congress, assigned to the position of Postmaster General and was on the drafting committee of the Declaration. He sought support abroad for the new Republic and was well thought of there for his wit, intelligence and skills in diplomacy.

His tireless work on the Constitution and his politcal acumen in bringing opposing forces together at the Federal Consitutional Convention of 1787 is considered exceptional statesmanship.

A Second Generation Statesman

John Quincy Adams, 1767-1848, was one of the second generation of statesmen that contributed much to the anchoring of America as a respected nation. He was the son of John and Abigail Adams and was a diplomat, not only in Washington's administration but in his father's as well. John Quincy Adams is known less for his tenure as sixth President of the United States (1825-1829), as he is for his scholarly and forthright statesmanship as Secretary of State under James Monroe's administration, where he had much to do with the articulation of the Monroe Doctrine.

Declaration of Independence

In Congress, July 4, 1776
The Unanimous Declaration of the Thirteen United States of America

When in the Course of human events, it becomes necessary for one people to dissolve the political bands which have connected them with another, and to assume among the Powers of the earth, the separate and equal station to which the Laws of Nature and of Nature's God entitle them, a decent respect to the opinions of mankind requires that they should declare the causes which impel them to the separation.

We hold these truths to be self-evident, that all men are created equal, that they are endowed by their Creator with certain unalienable Rights, that among these are Life, Liberty and the pursuit of Happiness. That to secure these rights, Governments are instituted among Men, deriving their just powers from the consent of the governed. That whenever any Form of Government becomes destructive of these ends, it is the Right of the People to alter or abolish it, and to institute new Government, laying its foundation on such principles and organizing its powers in such form, as to them shall seem most likely to effect their Safety and Happiness. Prudence, indeed, will dictate that Governments long established should not be changed for light and transient causes; and accordingly all experience hath shown, that mankind is more disposed to suffer, while evils are sufferable, than to right themselves by abolishing the forms to which they are accustomed. But when a long train of abuses and usurpations, pursuing invariably the same Object evinces a design to reduce them under absolute Despotism, it is their right, it is their duty, to throw off such Government, and to provide new Guards for their future security. --Such has been the patient sufferance of these Colonies; and such is now the necessity which constrains them to alter their former Systems of Government. The history of the present King of Great Britain is a history of repeated injuries and usurpations, all having in direct object the establishment of an absolute Tyranny over these States. To prove this, let Facts be submitted to a candid world.

He has refused his Assent to Laws, the most wholesome and necessary for the public good.

He has forbidden his Governors to pass Laws of immediate and pressing importance, unless suspended in their operation till his Assent should be obtained; and when so suspended, he has utterly neglected to attend to them.

He has refused to pass other Laws for the accommodation of large districts of people, unless those people would relinquish the right of Representation in the Legislature, a right inestimable to them and formidable to tyrants only.

He has called together legislative bodies at places unusual, uncomfortable and distant from the depository of their Public Records, for the sole purpose of fatiguing them into compliance with his measures.

He has dissolved Representative Houses repeatedly, for opposing with manly firmness his invasions on the rights of the people.

He has refused for a long time, after such dissolutions, to cause others to be elected; whereby the Legislative Powers, incapable of Annihilation, have returned to the People at large for their exercise; the State remaining in the mean time exposed to all the dangers of invasion from without, and convulsions within.

He has endeavoured to prevent the population of these States; for that purpose obstructing the Laws of Naturalization of Foreigners; refusing to pass others to encourage their migrations hither, and rasing the conditions of new Appropriations of Lands.

He has obstructed the Administration of Justice, by refusing his Assent to Laws for establishing Judiciary Powers.

He has made Judges dependent on his Will alone, for the tenure of their offices, and the amount and payment of their salaries.

He has erected a multitude of New Offices, and sent hither swarms of Officers to harass our people, and eat out their substance.

He has kept among us, in times of peace, Standing Armies without the Consent of our legislatures.

He has affected to render the Military independent of and superior to Civil Power.

He has combined with others to subject us to a jurisdiction foreign to our constitution, and unacknowledged by our laws; giving his Assent to their acts of pretended Legislation:

For quartering large bodies of armed troops among us:

For protecting them, by a mock Trial, from Punishment for any Murders which they should commit on the Inhabitants of these States:

For cutting off our Trade with all parts of the world:

For imposing taxes on us without our Consent:

For transporting us beyond Seas to be tried for pretended offences:

For abolishing the free System of English Laws in a neighboring Province, establishing therein an Arbitrary government, and enlarging its Boundaries so as to render it at once an example and fit instrument for introducing the same absolute rule into these Colonies:

For depriving us in many cases, of the benefits of Trial by Jury:

For taking away our Charters, abolishing our most valuable Laws, and altering fundamentally the Forms of our Governments:

For suspending our own Legislatures, and declaring themselves invested with Power to legislate for us in all cases whatsoever.

He has abdicated Government here, by declaring us out of his Protection and waging War against us.

He has plundered our seas, ravaged our Coasts, burnt our towns, and destroyed the lives of our people.

He is at this time transporting large armies of foreign mercenaries to compleat the works of death, desolation and tyranny, already begun with circumstances of Cruelty & perfidy scarcely paralleled in the most barbarous ages, and totally unworthy the Head of a civilized nation.

He has constrained our fellow Citizens taken Captive on the high Seas to bear arms against their Country, to become executioners of their friends and Brethren, or to fall themselves by their Hands.

He has excited domestic insurrections amongst us, and has endeavoured to bring on the inhabitants of our frontiers, the merciless Indian Savages whose known rule of warfare, is an undistinguished destruction of all ages, sexes and conditions.

In every stage of these Oppressions We have Petitioned for Redress in the most humble terms: Our repeated Petitions have been answered only by repeated injury. A Prince, whose character is thus marked by every act which may define a Tyrant, is unfit to be the ruler of a free people.

Nor have We been wanting in the attentions to our British brethren. We have warned them from time to time of attempts by their legislature to extend an unwarrantable jurisdiction over us. We have reminded them of the circumstances of our emigration and settlement here. We have appealed to their native justice and magnanimity, and we have conjured them by the ties of our common kindred to disavow these usurpations which, would inevitably interrupt our connection and correspondence. They too have been deaf to the voice of justice and of consanguinity. We must, therefore, acquiesce in the necessity, which denounces our Separation, and hold them, as we hold the rest of mankind, Enemies in War, in Peace Friends.

We, therefore, the Representatives of the united States of America, in General Congress, Assembled, appealing to the Supreme Judge of the world for the rectitude of our intentions, do, in the Name, and by authority of the good People of these Colonies, solemnly publish and declare, That these United Colonies are, and of Right ought to be Free and Independent States; that they are Absolved from all Allegiance to the British Crown, and that all political connection between them and the State of Great Britain, is and ought to be totally dissolved; and that as Free and Independent States, they have full power to levy War, conclude Peace, contract Alliances, establish Commerce, and to do all other Acts and Things which Independent States may of right do. And for the support of this Declaration, with a firm reliance on the Protection of Divine Providence, we mutually pledge to each other our Lives, our Fortunes and our sacred Honor.

John Hancock.	Charles Carroll of Carrollton.	Geo. Taylor.	Abra. Clark.
Button Gwinnett.	George Wythe.	James Wilson.	Josiah Bartlett.
Lyman Hall.	Richard Henry Lee.	Geo. Ross.	Wm. Whipple.
Geo. Walton.	Th. Jefferson.	Cæsar Rodney.	Saml. Adams.
Wm. Hooper.	Benj. Harrison.	Geo. Read.	John Adams.
Joseph Hewes.	Thos. H. Nelson, Jr.	Tho. M'Kean.	Robt. Treat Payne.
John Penn.	Francis Lightfoot Lee.	Wm. Floyd.	Elbridge Gerry.
Edward Rutledge.	Carter Braxton.	Phil. Livingston.	Step. Hopkins.
Thos. Heyward, Junr.	Robt. Morris.	Frans. Lewis.	William Ellery.
Thomas Lynch, Junr.	Benjamin Rush.	Lewis Morris.	Roger Sherman.
Arthur Middleton.	Benja. Franklin.	Richd. Stockton.	Sam'el. Huntington.
Samuel Chase.	John Morton.	Jno. Witherspoon.	Wm. Williams.
Wm. Paca.	Geo. Clymer.	Fras. Hopkinson.	Oliver Wolcott.
Thos. Stone.	Jas. Smith.	John Hart.	Matthew Thornton.

FREEDOM IS DEFENDED

When our founding fathers penned the Declaration of Independence they made many commitments. One was to baptize our fledgling nation with the waters of freedom, justice, and equality. Another was to create a democratic form of government which would allow Americans the ability to pursue their own dreams, as free men. These rights were to be inalienable; rights decreed not by man but by God.

Finally, America committed herself to the defense of these rights. A declaration of independence from Britain was viewed by the monarchy as nothing short of treason, and the colonies, like an unruly child, were to be punished and brought back into the imperial fold. Thus began the need for America to turn to her sons for protection.

From the first shots of the Revolutionary War to the final salvo of Desert Storm, Americans have answered the call to arms. We have done so to protect those same inalienable rights set forth over 200 years ago. The very reasons that we, as Americans, enjoy these rights is because we have given our very lives to protect them. We have done so with the conviction that our cause was just, honorable and blessed.

The extent of our conviction to defend these rights was evidenced by the one war we fought amongst ourselves, the Civil War. Over a hundred years have passed since that bloody confrontation, and America still pledges to defend the God-given right of people to live free, unencumbered by mandates from those with different ideologies. However, as long as there are people who force their will on others, America will stand as a barrier to defend not just the rights of our citizens, but those of other nations as well. We defend the right of all people to take part in the great experiment known as democracy. We do so with the same assurances that we are defending the rights of humankind as spelled out by God Himself.

War is pain. War is fear. War is death and destruction. War is also separation from one's family and friends. War gives insight into the darkest crevices of human emotion and mental being. But if War brings out the worst in us, it also brings forth the best in us—honor, duty, courage, camaraderie, unbelievable acts of heroism and self-sacrifice. War also brings forth a profound sense of faith, as God stands beside the soldier, sailor, airman and marine. Finally, when all vestiges of civilization have been stripped from us, it is an abiding faith in God that nurtures and sustains us, and once again, we know our cause is just. Rights are not kept without sacrifice, and we all owe much to our fallen soldiers who have insured the continuation of our rights with the ultimate sacrifice.

"We defend the right of all people to take part in the great experiment known as democracy."

War Between the States

The causes of war are usually many, and so is the case with the conflict that brought death to more Americans than any other war in our history. Slavery, of course, was an issue which uncovered political, economic, social and moral weaknesses of the still young republic. Sectionalism was growing however–even aside from the issue of slavery. South Carolina became the first to secede from the Union with the national election of Abraham Lincoln. Ten other states would eventually follow to form the Confederacy.

In the war of brother against brother, leaders and battlefields ring familiar as if an indelible part of the American consciousness: Lincoln, Davis, Jackson, Chancellorsville, Fredericksburg, McClellan, Hood, Hooker, Vicksburg, Antietam, Beauregard, Stuart, Bull Run, Gettysburg, Grant, Lee, Appomattox. And still today, the names of relatives who fought in the bloody contests of our Civil War, the names of the boys, volunteer or conscript, are spoken not just with a sense of sadness that it had to be, but also with a sense of honor that in that time and in this, the place we call America, principle was so esteemed.

"Let us have faith that right makes might, and in that faith let us to the end dare to do our duty as we understand it."

—*Abraham Lincoln*

G.A.R. veteran and young friend, circa 1930

Confederate infantryman

General Robert E. Lee

The Great War (1914-1918)

World War I was caused by an amalgam of territorial disputes set off by European imperialism and economic rivalries and fueled by rampant nationalism.

Germany joined with Austria-Hungary, followed by the Ottoman Empire and Bulgaria, among others, to form what was called the Central Powers. Serbia, Russia, France, Belgium, Great Britain and Italy, among other forces to follow, formed the Allied Forces. Along the Eastern and Western Fronts hundreds of thousands died in the trenches and on battlefields where tanks were first used and soldiers became the first victims of poison gas.

With the landing of the American Expeditionary Forces in France in June of 1917 came a great boost to allied morale and a power that could help end the war. The Central Powers were worn, beaten and disintegrating. A General Armistice was signed November 11, 1918. Very conserv-ative estimates counted at least 10 million dead and 20 million wounded.

The so-called "Great War" annihilated the flower of European manhood and changed the face of Europe. The United States would evermore be seen as a protector of liberty and defender of freedom worldwide.

A member of the American Expeditionary Force (AEF)

Uncle Sam

Some have attributed the actual name to one Samuel Wilson (1766-1854), who inspected army supplies and was nicknamed "Uncle Sam." The first use as a recruiting tool, however, was in World War I, when "Uncle Sam" became patriotism personified.

"And we shall fight for the things which we have always carried nearest to our hearts–for democracy, for the right of those who submit to authority to have a voice in their own governments, for the rights and liberties of small nations, for a universal dominion of right by such a concert of free people as shall bring peace and safety to all nations and make the world itself at last free." —*Woodrow Wilson*

Rosie the riveter

The marines raise the flag over Iwo Jima

Naval pilot

World War II (1939-1945)

As a great depression crossed the globe in the 1930's and as the peace settlements of World War I left unstable conditions abroad, Germany, Italy and Japan became re-committed to militarism under totalitarian regimes. Germany began occupation of all of Czechoslovakia and Italy overtook Albania. Britain and France began to seek allies and on September 3, 1939 they declared war on Germany as a result of Germany's invasion of Poland.

Although the U.S. was committed to neutrality it became necessary to protect her ships from German submarine attack in the Atlantic. Meanwhile Japan, without warning, attacked Pearl Harbor, the Phillipines and Malaya. On December 8, 1941 the U.S. declared war on Japan.

Figured into the inevitable devastation rendered in World War II are the terrible ramifications of modern warfare, especially nuclear weapons. And Hitler's attempt to exterminate the Jewish people was one of the most heinous crimes in the history of humanity.

American soldiers from communities all over our country joined in fighting unsurpassed aggression and monstrous evil. And, at home, everyone pitched in, women handling jobs that only men had done before, families sacrificing the basics so that the full power of U.S. industry could aid the war effort. Many soldiers gave their lives so that the forces of good would not be conquered and liberty would reign.

In those years of great turmoil and loss, the American way of life became defined by the virtues of courage and sacrifice.

Korea (1950-1953)

With the end of the Second World War, Korea was divided into U.S. (South) and Communist (North) occupied zones at the 38th parallel. In June of 1950 North Korean forces invaded South Korea. After the capture of Seoul, the southern capital, by Communist forces fighting was intensified and later returned to and remained at the 38th parallel. After much hardship on battlefield and negotiating table, an armistice was signed on July 27, 1953. The United States lost over 54,000 soldiers in fighting the advancement of Communist forces. We must not overlook our veterans of this era. Perhaps their courage and commitment is just now coming to fruition with the collapse of the Communist world.

Vietnam (1961-1973)

Following the defeat of French colonial powers in 1954 and rising up out of a Vietnamese civil war were the insurgent guerrilla warriors, the Viet Cong, whose political organization was known as the National Liberation Front. This

The helicopter replaced the horse in the cavalry and was instrumental in many life-saving evacuations of wounded. Those who did not return are memorialized forever on the "Wall" (inset), the Vietnam Veterans' Memorial in Washington, D.C.

force, combined with the North Vietnamese troops with a network of supplies from the Communist world opposed the South Vietnamese army which was supported economically and militarily by the U.S., along with token forces from other nations. The first American troops arrived in Vietnam in 1961 and by 1966 there were 190,000. By 1969, the number had reached 550,000. The devastating Tet offensive of 1968 showed the destructive aim of North Vietnam and Viet Cong forces, as well as, ultimately, the responsive power of the United States military. Peace negotiations expanded in 1969 and a troop withdrawal/air offensive strategy came into being with the newly-elected U.S. President Richard Nixon. A peace agreement was finally reached in January of 1973.

The Vietnam War was opposed by many U.S. citizens. But that opposition came to be translated into a neglectful, even hostile at times, attitude toward the veterans who served their country there so courageously. Our nation is still coming to grips with its involvement in Vietnam as with the treatment of her brave soldiers, over 50,000 of whom died defending democracy in the jungles of southeast Asia.

Desert Storm (January 1992)

Once again, the U.S. demonstrated its leadership role in the reaction to the invasion of Kuwait by Iraq. In a conflict lasting just over 100 hours and utilizing to a large extent allied air superiority, the Iraqi aggressors were driven from Kuwait. Ground forces numbered nearly 200,000 at one time in the preparation for the confrontation between Saddam Hussein's military and the combined forces of the United Nations.

United States reserve forces played a major role in the success of the military operation. Men and women with jobs and families left both to defend freedom in the desert of the middle east.

The troops at Desert Storm

THE AMERICAN SPIRIT IS CHALLENGED

The American spirit, from the native righteousness of the founding fathers to the civic consciousness of those who provide for present day soup kitchens, has been at every point in the great graph of its history, challenged by poverty, ignorance, subjugation of freedom and its own restless pioneer heritage.

America has ceaselessly struggled in the public and private sectors to eliminate poverty from her shores. The struggle goes on. Sometimes progress is too slow for us and in some cases our own programs have ended up engendering an underclass they were instituted to eliminate. But with problems that wrack the American heart, come ideas and instances of generosity wholly disposed to protecting the dignity of each individual human being.

For instance, America's commitment to the education of her citizenry has been exemplary. Working with the present day decline in objective moral standards, as seen in the dissolution of the family and the subsequent loss of stability and direction in children is a monumental effort. But in the rough of recent misguided efforts common to a secular society, diamonds glitter in the persons of parents and teachers given to imparting as best they can the basics of objective Judeo-Christian standards of conduct.

Never before in the history of mankind have so many people of varying cultures been so protected of their civil rights as in present day America. Visionaries such as Martin Luther King gave their lives to ensure the freedom of all people. But oppression has many faces and much work is left to do. Many, like the unborn, are still unprotected in what we hope will someday be a fully enlightened society where all human beings are seen as being made in the image and likeness of their Creator.

As the American heart yearns for solutions, so does it yearn for exploration. It always has and it always will. The pioneering impulse remains and, as the world has become smaller, space and its environs have become that much more attractive to the American psyche. It is hoped that knowledge of other worlds will foster a spirit of cooperation and constructive application of that knowledge at home. Those who have looked upon our planet earth from afar have been profoundly moved by the experience. Perhaps the same perspective will someday allow us to come closer to the Creator of the universe we so love to examine, and return to the heritage our forebears cherished.

"...a fully enlightened society where all human beings are seen as being made in the image and likeness of their Creator."

1908. A ten-year-old spinner at a cotton mill. She had been working in the mill for over a year at the time of the photograph.

The Social Ills of a Young Nation

Along with great progress, industrialization also brought with it unforeseen social ills. The factory system emerging from Britain in the early part of the 19th century took children from work within their families and other apprenticeships that regulated their activities to a cruel and oppressive situation in factories that would take many years to resolve.

The problem of child labor began to be addressed in the United States after the Civil War. Many and various attempts to relieve our nation's children of the burden of adult labor were defeated. The Supreme Courts of 1918 and 1922 declared child labor laws unconstitutional and a 1924 constitutional amendment passed Congress but did not have enough support in the states. It was not until 1938 with the first Labor Standards Act that minimum age labor standards came into being. Since that time, the United States has been more attentive than most other nations of the world to the welfare of its children, be it in the area of child labor, poverty and hunger, or education.

The Civil Rights of Our Citizenry

Since the time of slavery African Americans have struggled to achieve equality under the law. After the blight of slavery, segregation continued to inflict and oppress the black population of the United States, most of whom by the 1950's were third and fourth-generation American citizens.

It was in this decade that a leader arose from the pulpit of a Baptist church in Montgomery, Alabama. Martin Luther King, Jr., who in 1955 led a boycott of the Montgomery city bus lines, which were segregated, would become the most influential leader of the civil rights movement.

Rev. King's adherence to passive (non-violent) resistance as a strategy in the desegregation of America would lead to his arrest on many occasions but also to his being honored with the Nobel Peace Prize in 1964.

Perhaps no other American has done more to ensure the rights of an oppressed minority than Martin Luther King, Jr. His untimely death by an assassin's bullet in 1968 not only left the civil rights movement devoid of a spiritual leader but shocked the nation as a whole.

"I have a dream that...little children will one day live in a nation where they will not be judged by the color of their skin but by the content of their character"

from a speech by Dr. King, August 28, 1963

Though great progress has been made in the area of human rights for all American citizens, there is much left to do. When any of our citizens do not gain access to the liberties for which so many have fought so hard, the job is not done. The progress made, however, is a tribute to the ever-emerging Judeo-Christian sense of fairness and compassion for one's fellows that has been a part of the American spirit since the founding of our nation.

Coping With Tragedy

Even great nations experience social ills. The evidence of great virtue, however, is in the nation's response. Homelessness is today a great concern to our country. We must begin to define the homeless population more accurately. Some of our homeless choose to be where they are and therefore should elicit a response appropriate to the choices they have made. Others, however, are unfortunate victims of a failed national policy which attempted to place responsibility for our

mentally ill citizens at the local level. Our urban streets are now filled with those who should, for their own welfare, be institutionalized. And the high percentage of chemically dependent homeless, that is, alcohol and other drug addicts, should be treated yet another way. Different segments of the homeless population require different responses and personal accountability should always be in the forefront of our national, state and community policies concerning this difficult and complex problem.

Salvation Army soup kitchen

Always The Good Neighbor

Nearby tragedy one always finds the good of heart, seeking to alleviate pain and create hope in the lives of the unfortunate. America responds to tragedy like no other people. Good people become saintly when a neighbor is in need. Great sacrifice for others is common when disaster leaves any of our people without food, shelter, clothing or other basic needs. Such demonstrations of charity and generosity offer the afflicted hope; and with hope and faith, anything is possible. In these demonstrations of love we are also, as a people, continually reborn.

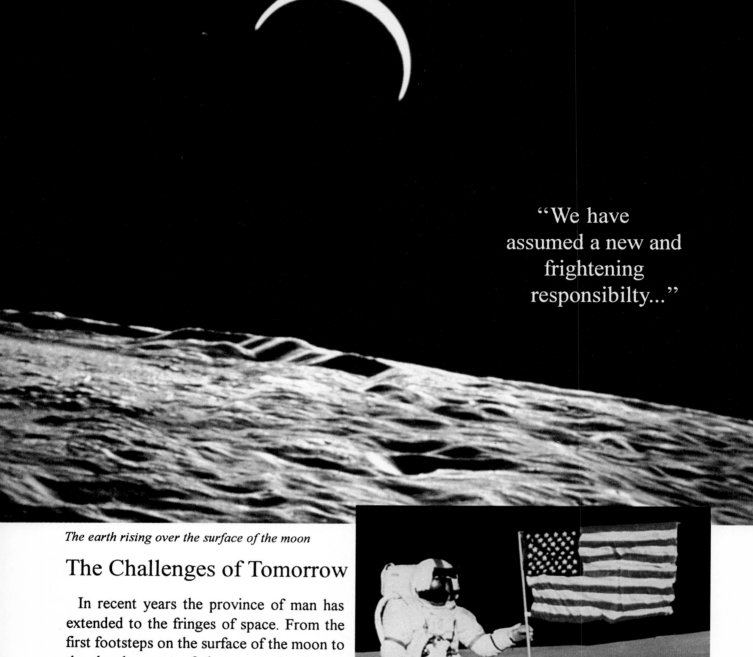

"We have
assumed a new and
frightening
responsibilty..."

The earth rising over the surface of the moon

The Challenges of Tomorrow

In recent years the province of man has extended to the fringes of space. From the first footsteps on the surface of the moon to the development of the space shuttle, we have placed ourselves in a new perspective–a perspective which has made us see more clearly our role in the universe.

Because we have seen the earth rise from far in space, we have been humbled in its fragile beauty. We have assumed a new and frightening responsibilty, not only of the stewardship of our own planet, but the love and care of our fellow man.

Planting the American flag

Our challenge then, as beneficiaries of the Judeo-Christian standard of conduct, is to recognize what our responsibilities are as moral beings, and to rise to the opportunities presented us to make our community (and our world) a better environment for us all.

FOUNDATIONS
OF
DEMOCRACY

There is nothing mysterious about the foundations of a healthy and strong democracy. The basic things expected by our people of their political and economic systems are simple.
They are:

★ equality of opportunity for youth and for others;

★ jobs for those who can work;

★ security for those who need it;

★ the ending of special privilege for the few;

★ the preservation of civil liberties for all;

★ the enjoyment of the fruits of scientific progress in a wider and constantly rising standard of living.

> Franklin D. Roosevelt
> message to the 77th Congress,
> 1941

GOD
IS
WORSHIPPED

In his famous "Farewell Address," George Washington said:

Of all the suppositions and habits which lead to political prosperity, religion and morality are indispensable supports. In vain would that man claim the tribute of Patriotism, who should labour to subvert these great pillars of human happiness, these firmest props of the duties of men and citizens.

Unfortunately, the "indispensable supports" of which our first President spoke are being called into question today. Under the guise of protecting religious freedom, some have sought, not only to eliminate all religious sentiment from public life, but also to ridicule religious expression even in private life. The great majority of American citizens, however, know that their country was founded upon Judeo-Christian principles as presented to us in the Ten Commandments and, as Washington continues,

"...reason and experience both forbid us to expect that National morality can prevail in exclusion of religious principle."

Even if religious principle is waning in government and public life, leaving the notion of "national morality" in question today, individual Americans and their families choose to express their religious sentiments unabashedly and with a commitment and passion uncommonly vigorous. We celebrate the life of the Church in America as we celebrate the religious impulse that is the backbone of our country.

"...religion and morality are indispensable supports."

John Wesley preaching, from a painting by William Hatherell

"...I have hallowed this house, which thou hast built, to put my name there for ever..."

—I Kings 9:3

The House of Worship

The word "church" comes from the Greek "kuraikon," meaning "belonging to the Lord." The house of Christian worship did not appear as a structure until the late third century, for before that time Christians worshipped secretly, mostly in private homes, to avoid persecution. Through the ages Byzantine, Romanesque, Gothic and Baroque architecture defined the structural look of the Christian house of worship. In the east as well as in the west, churches became the receptacle for great works of art such as stained glass scenes from scripture dedicated to the glory of God.

The simple, spired churches of the American Colonial period, however, were noted for their beauty and lack of ostentation. Many American churches of this style are still in use, inviting their congregations through the arched doorways to praise the Lord.

The synagogue of the Jewish tradition goes back to the Babylonian exile of the sixth century B.C. By the first century A.D. a familiar structure served as the cultural and religious center of Jewish life. Although at a later period the Jewish synagogue became associated more strictly with religious services, of late it has recaptured its meaning of old by becoming once again the social and cultural center of Jewish life as well as the edifice in which ancient but meaningful religious rites of Judaism are conducted.

"O magnify the Lord with me, and let us exalt His name together."

—*Psalm 34:3*

Worshipers in Washington, D.C. church, circa 1940

The Forms of Worship

In our nation we see a multitude of forms and styles of worship. Some forms emphasize more the charismatic manner of embracing with one's whole being the presence of the Holy Spirit, while others lean toward the contemplative elements of liturgical rites. But most ways of worshipping God express the notion of human subservience to a Supreme Being which guides us and will, if called upon, lead us onto the path of faith.

A young man kneels at prayer.

‘‘For where
two or three
are gathered
together
in my name,
there am I
in the midst
of them.’’

—*Matthew 18:20*

Contemporary churchgoers

1940's congregation

THE FAMILY LIVES ON

The American family has been forced to weather many attacks in the last 50 years; perhaps none so devastating as the sexual revolution of the 1960's. Since that time promiscuity has come to be implicitly accepted in many forums, especially in the "sound bytes" and visual images pouring forth from our national electronic media. And when sexuality is separated from its loving foundation in the marriage contract, something begins to happen to the family. That foundation begins to crumble and the Judeo-Christian emphasis on commitment to others is gradually replaced with a deceptive, destructive and self-centered hedonism that leaves so many good people lost, yearning for the security that can come only from a loving God and a loving family.

It is within the benevolent confines of the family that we first learn the objective, Judeo-Christian standards of conduct that will enable us to survive in a world more and more given to testing the endurance of the human spirit. How to experience the fullness of joy and cope with the pain of sadness and grief; how to encounter prejudice and scorn with a head held high; how to value good work for good purposes; all of these lessons begin in the course of family life. And if that family life is threatened by secular notions of individual fulfillment at almost any cost, the paradoxical effect will be little, if any, individual fulfillment, accompanied ultimately by a fatalistic world view.

But the American family lives on. We are fighting its dissolution with all our might. Parents struggle to simplify their lives, returning to the Judeo-Christian values that they come to find still work as well now as in the time of the Old Testament heroes and heroines and in the time of Christ. Right is still right, and wrong is still wrong. And although the American family is under attack, there are, on every street in every town, in every state in the nation, mothers, fathers, children; grandparents, aunts, uncles; cousins, friends and familiar faces, pulling together in good times and in bad, laughing, crying, arguing and making up. There are families separated by time and distance who nevertheless find ways of communicating their abiding love. There are families who know that they are the strength of American citizenship, the very essence of our American way of life. Let us look to those faces for our hope. Let us look to them to witness the love that has been passed to us from our great Judeo-Christian heritage.

"...they are the strength of American citizenship..."

84

"Give me your tired, your poor,
Your huddled masses yearning to breathe free,
The wretched refuse of your teeming shore,
Send these, the homeless, tempest-tossed to me,
I lift my lamp beside the golden door!"

–Emma Lazarus (1849-1887).
Used as an inscription on the Statue of Liberty.

The American Family

Husbands & Wives, Brothers & Sisters

Papas, Mamas and Grands!

THE COMMUNITY SURVIVES

Just as families are the cornerstone of healthy communities so communities are the cornerstone of a healthy nation. Where families fall apart, so do communities; therefore the community has quite a vested interest in the well-being of the families that make up its fabric.

Families support the community through churches, hospitals, schools and businesses. Good communities respond by attempting to serve the welfare of each family, from the cradle to the grave, and from the most elemental of needs like food, health care, and housing, to those services so important to the life of the family and provided by funeral homes, financial institutions, eating establishments and the many other fine merchants and professional people who offer much needed goods and services, to name a few.

Even in the midst of large cities, people will gather into smaller groups in frenetic attempts to establish spiritual intimacy and friendship. People strive, whether consciously or unconsciously, to become caretakers for one another. The Judeo-Christian tradition is the story of that kind of fraternal response. We are, like it or not, inexplicably drawn to each other and, as children of a loving God, we will seek each other out for allegiance, compassion and mutually beneficial relationships.

And that is as it should be. America is a nation of communities that form an interdependent chain. If our communities and families remain strong and supportive of each other, then the nation will follow.

Our communities celebrate our births, grieve our deaths, and link arms with us for the journey in between. Let us commit ourselves to their worth and continue to support them. And let us bathe in the rich images of community that follow.

*"We are,
like it or not,
inexplicably
drawn to
each other..."*

In times of need . . .

Local churches and synagogues are still the heart of the community.

Serving the medical needs of the community

Funeral homes serve families with dignity in times of sorrow and loss.

. . . the community is ready to serve

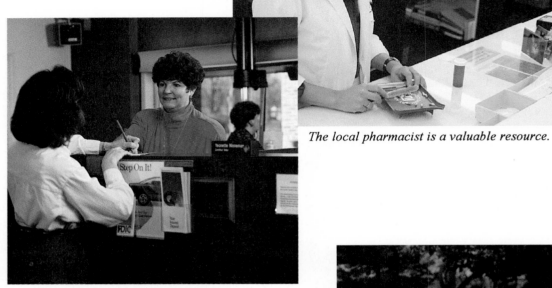

The local pharmacist is a valuable resource.

A personal banker helps with financial needs.

To serve and protect is the aim of the local police officer.

Many retail merchants become community leaders.

. . . and families
return their support

Saluting the flag in the Mott Street Industrial School, New York, circa 1892

The Children's Declaration

We, the children of the United States of America, born of farmers, storekeepers, clerks, ironworkers, artists—on the plains, in the mountains, in the villages and in the cities, do hereby pledge our faith in the future. We have this faith because we are the future.

We are of all colors, creeds, and races. We have studied our country's historic documents, and we know that these are more than paper and parchment and words, and that we, the future, must keep their truths close to our hearts and make them live. We stand on the threshold of destiny in a world where ideas good and evil engulf us, to be boldly accepted or rejected. We are children, but unlike those of 1776, we can see and hear in our homes the actual sounds and visions of history at the moment it is made.

We know well the meaning of sacrifices made by our fathers, brothers, and neighbors on the battlefields. We are not afraid of things to come. We believe that the God of our great, great grandfathers is just as near today; and we subscribe to this declaration, knowing that it is as real as our resolve to be free.

—*R. E. Beauchamp*

United States of America...

The resolve to be free continues.